LIVING INTO DEATH, DYING INTO LIFE

A CHRISTIAN THEOLOGY OF DEATH AND LIFE ETERNAL

D0706405

PETER C. PHAN

lectio

Lectio Publishing, LLC
Hobe Sound, FL

www.lectiopublishing.com

Cover design by Linda Wolf
Edited by Eric Wolf

ISBN 978-0-9898397-7-8
Library of Congress Control Number: 2014954415

Published by Lectio Publishing, LLC
on the Solemnity of All Saints, 2014

Hobe Sound, Florida 33455
www.lectiopublishing.com

CONTENTS

CONTENTS

PREFACE

This book originates as a series of twelve lectures on what is referred to in theological parlance as "eschatology" commissioned by *Now You Know Media*, an audio and video publishing company based in Rockville, Maryland, U.S.A., which produces audio programs on Catholic matters. By eschatology is meant the theology of the "Last Things" (*eschata*), namely, death and the realities after death.

The twenty-minute length of time allotted to each taped lecture did not allow a comprehensive treatment of the themes under consideration. This limitation however turned out to be a blessing since it forced me to focus on what is, from the Christian perspective, strictly essential. The book version gave me the opportunity to expand what I have said in the lectures, but I have decided not to lengthen it too much. Each of the twelve themes could be the subject of book-length treatises, and many theologians have written huge and learned tomes on each of them, complete with scholarly apparatuses of notes and bibliographical references. I have learned much from these writings, but have chosen not burden my text with references to the literature on the subject, except in very few places. These are de rigueur in the academy, not least to forestall the charge of plagiarism, but they tend to distract the kind of readers I have in mind.

Eschatology has been a constant concern of my scholarly endeavors. Indeed, my first doctoral dissertation deals with the eschatological vision of the Russian Orthodox theologian Paul Evdokimov, and my second with that of the German Catholic theologian Karl Rahner. Even my third deals with aspects of eschatology. But there is an existential difference between writing on death and dying in one's early thirties and doing the same when intimations of one's mortality are daily occurrences. Then death was someone else's, now it is *mine*. Then the afterlife was an object for scholarly reflections, now it is a reality to *live* everyday. Then heaven and hell were theological possibilities for all, now either is the destination for *me* at the end of my earthly journey. Then the return of Christ in glory to judge the quick and the dead was imagined as a future event at the end of time, trillions of years away, now it is an *imminent* act of God's judgment, anticipated in fear and trembling, but also hoped for in trust and confidence in God's infinite mercy. Then life was deathless existence, now it is *living into death*. Then dying is the end of everything, now it is *dying into life*.

Living into Death, Dying into Life, the title of this book, expresses both my own hope and the perspective in which the book is written. In a real sense, its primary targeted reader is none other than myself, trying to put into words the meaning and purpose of my own life, in the gathering darkness of its evening. I do hope however that it will also be of help to those who struggle with the enigma, or better still, mystery of life. The mention of "mystery" is not an intellectual copout or an attempt at obfuscation but an acknowledgment that life, death, and what follows after death, if anything follows at all, are not puzzles or problems to which empirically verifiable answers and testable solutions can be provided, with the help of science, or from a secret source of divine revelation. Rather "under-standing" the mystery of death and life after death requires a "standing-under," that is, an immersion in life, whose meaning cannot be stated beforehand but can only be discovered in the living of life itself. How we die is how we live, and how we live is how we die, each and every day.

During the composition of this book several of my dear friends preceded me in their journeys to God—their *itinerarium mentis ad Deum*—to use the title of Saint Bonaventure's celebrated work. May the angels carry them, and the brother of a friend of mine who took his own life in its prime, to their eternal home, into the company of the Triune God, whose ever-forgiving love is infinitely greater than our hearts, and in the fellowship with all the saints. To their memories this little book is dedicated. Till we all meet again. Or, as Nana Mouskouri sings: "Till the wild rose blooms again."

1

REALITY AND IMAGINATION

HOW DO WE KNOW AND TALK ABOUT THE AFTERLIFE?

The twelve chapters you are going to read deal with what was once called the "Last Things" (Latin: *De Novissimis*), that is, the realities occurring at the end of life, namely, death and dying, and those occurring in the afterlife, mainly, individual judgment, purgatory, hell, heaven, the resurrection, the general judgment, and the end of the world. The theological term for the treatment of these Last Things is "eschatology"—a term derived from two Greek words: *eschata* and *logos*—meaning discourse on the last things.

At the outset, I should perhaps issue a warning: Let the buyer beware (*caveat emptor*)! I suspect that most buyers would pick up this little book in the hope of finding *information* on and *answers* to some issues about life after death that have bothered them. They want, I presume, to *know* more about the Last Things, for example, what our life after death looks like, whether there will be a "rapture," whether there will be "Armageddon," what kinds of body they will get after the resurrection, whether with their risen bodies they will be able to enjoy the pleasures of eating, drinking and sex, whether they will be able to be reunited with friends and family, when the world will end, when and how Jesus will come again, what kinds of torture those in hell will be punished with, whether heaven will be like a never-ending party, and a host of other questions of this sort. Unfortunately, I must say that after reading this book they will not *know* more (perhaps will know even less) about these issues than they do now (note the emphasis on "know"). Potential buyers of this book looking for clear answers to these and similar questions will be sorely disappointed.

Contrary to, say, a course on biology or physics, in which data can be gathered and theses empirically tested and verified, and therefore progress in *knowledge* can be measured, quantified, even graded, in eschatology appeal cannot be made to empirical data in defense of what is being said. For example, when discussing dying, heaven or hell, I can't say: "Trust me, been there, done that." Were this true, I wouldn't be around writing this book, or if I were, it would be a very different sort of book, very likely a best-seller, offering detailed first-hand knowledge of the afterlife!

There is therefore a basic preliminary question about whether we *know* the Last Things, and if so, *by what method*, and how to *talk* about them. Obviously, thanks to modern medicine, we do know something about dying as a physiological act. Of this we can therefore speak with a measure of certainty. But of the *meaning* of death and above all, of what occurs *after* death, we do not and cannot have factual information at our disposal. As a consequence, our language about them cannot be that of a scientific description or a journalistic report.

Rather, as will be seen throughout the book, the language about the Last Things thrives on metaphor, poetry and analogy. Its purpose is not to impart new information on the afterlife derived from sacred books or a secret revelation but to arouse and nurture human hope about the future so that driven and energized by that hope, we can work toward a better world for all humanity and even the cosmos itself. Of the three theological virtues, that is, faith, hope and charity, it is hope that lies at the heart of eschatology.

However, there is no doubt that this kind of poetic and hope-filled language is liable to the charge that Christian eschatology weaves a fairy tale, or worse, to paraphrase Karl Marx, concocts an opium to lull the oppressed mass into a docile submission to the exploitative powers and an obedient acceptance of their fate as God's will and into waiting for their rewards in heaven that will never come. It is therefore necessary right from the start to clarify the nature of eschatological knowledge, the method by which we claim to "know" about the afterlife, and the kind of language that must be used to speak about it. This will be the theme of this chapter. The remaining eleven chapters discuss the realities often asked about when dealing with the afterlife. I beg for the reader's forbearance for this introductory chapter which may sound remote from the information they seek about what happens after death. Despite its seeming abstractness, what will be said here is of extreme importance for the rest of the book, as most misunderstandings of the afterlife arise from mistaking the imaginative language of eschatology for a factual description of what happens after death.

Before delving into issues concerning death and eternal life I would like to highlight four general features of the book. First, the titles of the chapters are phrased as questions—deliberately so—to highlight the tentative nature of my reflections and to invite further explorations. Second, the perspective from which I reflect on the afterlife is Christian, and more specifically, Roman Catholic. But I am speaking neither in the name of nor for the Catholic Church; I am not entitled nor am I inclined to do so. If you just want to know the official teaching of the Catholic Church about the Last Things, you can consult the 1994 *Catechism of the Catholic Church*, paragraphs 988-1050, and if you are in a hurry, peruse the summary in paragraphs 1051-1060. Fortunately, the text is brief; unfortunately, to understand it well requires a quite lengthy commentary. This book may be viewed as my personal commentary on these articles of the *Catechism*. Third, though my standpoint is Christian, in our contemporary world, where religious pluralism is a pervasive challenge yet also an enriching opportunity, it is necessary to do Christian theology in dialogue with other religions in order to learn from them. Consequently I will make frequent references to the beliefs and practices of other or "non-Christian" religions. Fourth, my approach to eschatology is thoroughly this-worldly; that is, it is not geared toward satisfying intellectual curiosity about the mysteries of the afterlife but to spell out the practical implications of the Last Things for our living on this Earth. That is the subtext of the title of this book: *Living into Death, Dying into Life.*

Can We Know About the Afterlife?

We live in the scientific age when "knowing" means observing data, formulating hypotheses, testing theories, and applying the resulting knowledge to practical fields. While it is generally acknowledged that the observer's theoretical bias is necessarily implicated in all these processes, objectivity remains the gold standard, and when experimental verification and scientific proof are lacking, the knowledge thus obtained is not counted as real knowledge but is dismissed as mere conjecture, pure speculation, or baseless superstition.

This epistemological framework is often inadvertently imported into theological discourse, and as a result, theologians are expected to come up with, or are assumed to provide, irrefutable and verifiable proofs for their assertions. However, empirical and rational proofs are in principle not available in matters pertaining to God. Were our knowledge of God reducible to scientific proofs, the God thus known would not be God but only an object, albeit the greatest, among other objects, the highest thing on the top rung of the cosmic ladder of things, the first link in the chain of links, the first cause in a series of causes. Such a god is an idol and would not be worthy of our irrevocable commitment in faith, hope, and love. Put differently, God is not a puzzle to be solved but a mystery, and more precisely, not a mystery but *the* Absolute Mystery, whom we come to know as the Being of infinite love. Our knowledge of such God must be consummated in praise, thanksgiving, and silent adoration.

Furthermore, it is to be noted that in the Christian tradition, knowledge of God is first of all not an achievement of human reasoning but a gift that is included in God's gracious self-revelation. Consequently, theology is the thinking activity in, with, by, and for the community of the women and men who have appropriated this self-gift of God in faith, hope, and love. It is rooted in faith and not only in reason. This does not mean that reason and faith are mutually incompatible. On the contrary, they are as it were the two lungs with which we breathe spiritually, the two wings with which we fly toward God. In doing theology we seek to use both reason and faith since both are God's gifts. Using one without the other would deprive us of the whole panoply of rich resources at our disposal. Relying on reason alone (rationalism), which is the temptation of modernity, often leads to skepticism and even nihilism. On the other hand, using faith alone (fideism), which is the pitfall of fundamentalism, turns the community of believers into a self-enclosed sect and a religious ghetto.

Do we then know anything about death and dying and the afterlife? The answer is a definitive yes, but with an all-important caveat: not by reason alone, nor by faith alone, but rather with reason illumined by faith and with faith supported by reason. By means of scientific and philosophical reason we do obtain some reliable— indeed quite useful—knowledge about death and dying and the immortality of the human soul; this knowledge based on reason alone is however quite limited and is subjected to continual revision. The medical sciences can describe the physiological processes of dying, and psychology can chart the various emotional stages a dying person goes through. Philosophical reasoning can argue for the survival of an element of the human person called "soul." But these fields of knowledge cannot provide the full meaning of death and dying and of the destiny of the individual person, the human community, and the cosmos. This meaning is available only through a different mode of knowing, one that is operative in what is called divine revelation, or more generally, religion. This mode of knowing does not supplant, much less destroy, scientific knowledge and human reason. Rather it expands and enriches them with new insights and understandings. To put it in St. Thomas Aquinas's celebrated formula, grace does not destroy nature but perfects it.

But this religious knowledge is not of the type that empirical sciences provide by means of their research methodologies. No doubt scientific knowledge, resulting in spectacular inventions and technologies, has brought immense improvement to the living conditions of a great part of humanity. In spite of its unimaginable progress and undeniable benefits, there is an inherent limitation to this kind of technologically-based knowledge: it is utterly powerless in resolving specifically *human* problems, which include but are more than biological, economic, social, political, and medical ones. Medical doctors, for instance, can help heal diseases but they cannot say anything *qua medical doctors* about the purpose of life and the meaning of death in general, much less the purpose of the life and the meaning of the death of *this* patient under their care. It would be obscene for them to say to the dying person, or to his or her loved ones, that there will hopefully be in the near future more effective medications and better medical procedures to prevent death. And even if science can deep-freeze the bodies of those who have died of an incurable disease in the hope of producing a future cure (cryonics) or prolong life forever, there is still the basic question to be faced, in principle unsolvable by science: why on earth and what for? It is here that a different kind of knowledge, no less important and useful than empirical knowledge, is needed, one that comes from the so-called human sciences such as literature, psychology, philosophy, the arts, and above all, religious studies and theology.

This recourse to channels of knowledge other than unaided or pure reason is widely done in what we refer to as world religions. Hinduism, for instance, appeals to what has been "heard" (*sruti*) from divine revelation and recorded in its sacred books, especially the Vedas, and "remembered" (*smirti*) in human but authoritative tradition. Buddhism attributes great authority to the teachings of the historical Buddha, namely, Siddhārtha Gautama (the *dharma*), as well as the *sutras* [writings] of later masters. Judaism is based on God's revelation as recorded in the Tanakh (the Hebrew Bible) and interpreted in the Talmud. Islam derives its teachings from the Word of God that is the Qur'an and from the Sunnah that reports the sayings and deeds of the Prophet Muhammad.

It is very important that this religious knowledge not be seen as a competitor to science, able to provide the *information* on the afterlife that science cannot deliver. Its purpose is not to *supplement* or *complete* the scientific information with *additional* information derived from secret and sacred sources. It cannot in principle do this, because it does not operate by the same principles and methods. Rather, religious knowledge about death and the afterlife aims at helping people "live to death"—to live in the knowledge that dying is an inherent part of living—and "die to life"—to die as an act of loving hope and trust in God's promise of eternal life.

For Christians, God's self-revelation in words and deeds is made known in the history of Israel and supremely in the life, ministry, death, and resurrection of Jesus of Nazareth. As recorded in the Bible and interpreted in Tradition, God's revelation remains for Christians the authoritative source of our knowledge of God and life after death. Again, it bears repeating that this divine revelation neither negates nor abolishes what can be known from reason. On the contrary, the knowledge of God and the afterlife that can be obtained by means of reason and the teachings of other religions complements and enriches what we know about them through the Jewish-Christian tradition. However, as Christians we confess and acknowledge that our knowledge of God and the afterlife is derived, albeit not exclusively, from Jesus' teachings. More specifically, what we Christians can know about death and life after death is based on what we have learned about what happened to Jesus himself during and after his death. Strictly speaking, Christian eschatology is nothing more than an extrapolation of Jesus' death and afterlife to the death and the afterlife of all human beings. If you permit me a theological jargon, eschatology is the "Christologization of anthropology."

How Do We Speak About the Afterlife?

Simple as this formula may sound, it is far from easy to determine exactly what happened to Jesus in and especially after his death and to speak about it in a way that does not smack of mythology and fairytale. Part of the problem is that, as I have noted above, we today are deeply habituated to the language of the empirical sciences, namely, that of exact description, classification, measurement, quantification, and verification. As a result, we tend to read texts literally, or more precisely, literalistically, except perhaps works of fiction and poetry. On the other hand, we may be so bored with the descriptive language of science that we read everything as mere metaphor or linguistic convention. Thus, in this intellectual climate our language has become either univocal, that is, every word is taken to have the same meaning in all cases, or equivocal, that is, no word is taken to have the same meaning in different cases.

Our world then is either totally flat and one-dimensional, where every word has but one and same meaning, or totally variegated and multi-dimensional, where the same word has completely different and unrelated meanings in different contexts. In the former case, we tend to be fundamentalistic, taking each and every biblical assertion about the afterlife as a scientific description or journalistic report of events that will happen to us after death. In the latter case, we end up in total skepticism, regarding what the Bible says about the afterlife as no more than interesting and even entertaining stories, which perhaps an enterprising movie producer can dramatize into a money-making blockbuster, but which have nothing meaningful to tell us because they belong to a totally fictional world, unrelated to ours.

Because of this scientistic (not scientific) and empiricist (not empirical) mindset, our imagination is stunted, and our language dull.

On our way to achieve technological mastery, we have lost the analogical imagination—the ability to see and think *otherwise*—which allows us to perceive connections and correlations among things that are at first sight totally unrelated, to apprehend both similarities and differences among disparate realities, to see things not simply as they are but also as they are *not* and *not yet*. Analogical imagination is what makes poets, artists, and theologians. They trade in metaphors, images and symbols because the realities they perceive cannot be expressed in conventional and circumscribed language. Theirs is the multi-dimensional and polyvalent speech of analogy which refuses to be straitjacketed by both the univocal and equivocal languages which can only either affirm or deny. On the contrary, the analogical language does three things at once: it *affirms* and *denies* and *transcends* every utterance. At the heart of analogy is the protest against every limitation in human knowledge and speech. In analogical language words still refer to things but they also point to the wider shores of wisdom dimly espied. Analogical language is a yearning for the unseen and the impossible and a stretching out to the infinite. Its lifeblood is hope in the future, and hence it is the language par excellence of eschatology.

A paradigmatic example of this hope-filled, eschatological language is a text from a letter of the apostle Paul. In his First Letter to the Thessalonian Christians, Paul writes about the fate of those who have died before the return of Christ. Paul and the Thessalonians expect that they would still be alive at the return of Christ in glory. What will happen then to those who are already dead? the Thessalonians ask. Would they be at a disadvantage compared with those who were still alive? In response, Paul says: "We who are alive, who are left until the coming of the Lord, will by no means precede those who have died. For the Lord himself, with a cry of command, with the archangel's call and with the sound of God's trumpet, will descend from heaven, and the dead in Christ will rise first. Then we who are alive, who are left, will be caught up in the clouds together with them to meet the Lord in the air, and so will be with the Lord forever" (1 Thess 4:15-17).

I will come back to this (in)famous text later, when I speak of the resurrection of the dead in chapter 8. Here I simply note that those who read it literalistically, both fundamentalists and skeptics, will have a field day with it. The skeptics will ask, with a smirk: Which language will the archangel use to make his call; what kind of material "God's trumpet" is made of; will Jesus descend from heaven in a supersonic vehicle; and will the dead sprout wings to fly up to meet him in the clouds? Undaunted by these sarcasms, fundamentalists will worry instead about tribulation, rapture, the thousand-year reign with Christ, the war against the Antichrist, and other phantasmagoric stuffs that make Tim LaHaye and Jerry B. Jenkins, the authors of the sixteen-volume novel *Left Behind*, multimillionaires. If we do not however take Paul's text literalistically but imaginatively, how should we understand its peculiar language and images in such a way that we take Paul's teaching about the resurrection of the dead and the return of Christ in glory seriously and yet will not be entrapped in the distracting and irrelevant issues that bedevil the fundamentalistic reading of the text? The answer, in a word, is analogy.

How Should We Interpret the Bible, Especially Its Eschatological Texts?

This leads us to the last issue of our first chapter: How can we read the Scripture, especially those texts on death and eternal life, rightly? Since the Bible is a historical, literary and revelatory text, we have to read it under these three perspectives.

First, because the Bible is a *historical* document, we must apply the *historical critical* method in order to ascertain what the author intends to say with his or her words. To do this task well, we begin with *textual criticism*. Because the Bible is an ancient text, or more precisely, a collection of "books" with multiple "authors," we need to determine whether a certain text is authentic or apocryphal, that is, whether it is written by the person alleged to have written it, and how accurately it has been copied and transmitted. (There were no photocopying machines then!) In a few places the manuscript (which is not made of acid-free paper!) is so corrupted that we have to reconstruct the text from other sources, and guess the meaning as accurately as we can. Sometimes there are variants of the same text in different manuscripts, and so we have to choose the most likely one. Next, we try to discern the possible influence of one text upon another, especially when there are different accounts of the same story (*source criticism*). For example, Matthew, Mark and Luke (the so-called Synoptic Gospels) are so similar to each other that we may ask: Who copies whom? (Today they would be charged with plagiarism since they do not cite their sources!)

Then we investigate the origin and history of the oral traditions before they were written down, the communities in which this process took place, and the various literary genres which the writer adopted to express himself (*form criticism*). Examining the literary forms of a text is essential in determining its meaning. For example, the text of Paul cited above is clearly not a journalistic report nor a realistic description of the end of the world—after all, the return of Jesus and the resurrection of the dead have not yet occurred; consequently it would be wrong-headed to read the Pauline text in this vein. The question to ask is: What literary genre is being adopted in this particular text? Contemporary biblical scholars suggest that it is the apocalyptic genre which, in both the canonical and apocryphal literatures, has its own peculiar language, style, and narrative mode.

The last part of historical criticism is *redaction criticism*, in which we try to identify the stages of the composition of the Bible by its authors and the creative role of the writers in editing, combining, and shaping the traditions they inherit. In short, in the first stage of trying to decipher the meaning of the Bible, we use the text as a *window* through which we look at *the world behind the text*.

Secondly, because the Bible is also a *literary* work, arguably the most widely read in world literature, it is necessary to apply *literary criticism* to understand it. We must ask what the authors intend to do with and for the readers, and how well they accomplish their goals. More specifically, since the Bible is a book of witness to God's words and deeds in history, we ask how well it does this task of transmitting God's self-revelation to us by analyzing its use of words and language, metaphors and images, literary forms and tropes, style and rhetorical strategies. A variety of methods and techniques have been used for this purpose. Some scholars have examined the Bible as a book of stories (*narrative criticism*); others, its art of persuasion (*rhetorical criticism*); others, its use of parables (*parable research*); others, its use of the letter genre (*epistolary analysis*); and still others, its impact upon the readers (*reader-response criticism*).

In this second phase of biblical interpretation, the Bible is seen as a *mirror in which the reader discovers herself or himself*. The focus is placed on the world *in* or *of* the text. When readers see themselves mirrored in the Bible, the Bible reveals a new way of being, a different possibility of existence that they must accept or reject. Again, coming back to Paul, what he is interested in is to keep the Thessalonians always ready, on their toes as it were, for the return of Christ, the Parousia, because, as he puts it, "the day of the Lord will come like the thief in the night" (1 Thess 4:2). So, if we today, when reading Paul's letter, see ourselves mirrored in the Thessalonians, we are similarly urged to stand on our toes and get ready for Christ's imminent return in glory, even if we, like the Thessalonians, are not seeing all the signs of it.

Thirdly, since the Bible is also a *sacred* book, a book that records God's self-revelation, it must also be read as Word of God, or more precisely, the Word of God in human words. Its purpose is not simply to instruct us about God and God's activities but to *transform* and *save* us. Thus the reader must personally *appropriate* the meaning of the Bible and in this way come to own its ideal meaning. Furthermore, since the Bible is a book of, by, and for the church, we must read it as a community of Christian believers, under the guidance of the Holy Spirit and following the Tradition of interpretation by the bishops, theologians, and indeed, the whole body of the faithful. In this third stage we focus not on the worlds *behind* and *in* the Bible but the world *in front of* it, that is, the new way of being and acting that the Bible proposes to us for our salvation.

There are then three steps in the process of deciphering the meaning of the Bible: first, *exegesis*, in order to understand the world *behind* the text; second, *criticism*, to understand the world *in* the text; and third, *hermeneutics*, to understand the world *in front of* the text. This triple process of interpreting the Bible is not performed by an individual in isolation, in a library as it were, but in the community of fellow believers, not simply for personal intellectual enrichment but for the total transformation of oneself and the world.

This three-step process of interpretation must be applied especially to the biblical texts that refer to the "Last Things" or eschatology, which are generally the hardest to interpret. As mentioned above, fundamentalists tend to take them literalistically, as factual reports of things to come; on the other hand, liberals reject them out of hand as fairytale. Ironically, despite their diametrically opposite theologies, liberals and conservatives share a common error, and that is, they take the eschatological texts of the Bible at their face values, and fail to take into account the worlds *behind*, *in*, and *in front of* these eschatological texts.

In summary, as Christians we do know something about death, dying, and above all life after death, as revealed to us in the life, death, and resurrection of Jesus. Eschatology is nothing more than extrapolating what has happened to Jesus in his death and after his death (his resurrection) to all human beings ("the Christologization of anthropology"). To speak of these realities adequately, there is the need of the analogical imagination and the analogical, not univocal or equivocal, language. Throughout the following chapters we will have the opportunities to look at the various biblical texts on death and dying and what lies after death, and will attempt to provide the most likely interpretations of them, taking them seriously but not literalistically, and appropriating their meanings to guide our living and dying. To arrive at the meanings of these

biblical texts requires a painstaking and complex process of interpretation (hermeneutics), involving various "criticisms" as required
by the nature of the Bible as a historical, literary, and sacred text.
In this hermeneutical process we try to discover the worlds *behind*,
of, and *in front of* the Bible, the Word that God delivered to the
saints in times past and still speaks to us today, as we journey in
hope toward the Absolute Mystery of Infinite Love.

2

DEATH AND DYING

END OR BEGINNING?

One of the deep ironies of our time is that medically, we now have more scientific information than ever on how dying occurs as a physiological process, and yet culturally, we also are more than ever reluctant to talk about it. On the one hand, there has been an exponential growth in scientific knowledge about death and dying. There is an interdisciplinary study of death called "thanatology" which investigates the physiological, medical, psychological, sociological, and legal aspects of death. We can now distinguish between cardiac arrest, brain death, clinical death, and legal death. Thanks to the work of psychologists and psychiatrists such as Elisabeth Kübler-Ross, we can discern the various stages that the dying person, and most often the grieving survivors as well, go through; namely, denial, anger, bargaining, depression, and acceptance, albeit not necessarily all of them, nor in that particular sequence. There has also been developed a medical specialty called "hospice and palliative medicine" which is dedicated to the symptom management, relief of suffering, and end-of-life care. Indeed, American interest in death and dying has been so extensive in recent decades that sociologists have referred to it as "the death awareness movement."

On the other hand in spite, or perhaps because, of this explosion of medical information on death and dying, there is a general tendency, notably in the West, to avoid facing death as *my* personal act, the fact that *I* shall die. Scholars can talk with considerable expertise about death in general, but shy away from thinking about *their own dying*. Death is always someone else's, never *mine*. This is in part because we can only hear the news of somebody else's death and may be shocked if it is sudden, or relieved if it is preceded by unbearable pains, and mourn it deeply, but by definition I cannot receive news of or report my own death (unless, like the report of Mark Twain's, it is vastly premature). Perhaps there is something instinctual about our refusal to contemplate the reality of our own death and to imagine what it feels like.

I Will Die

There is no doubt however that our contemporary cultural and societal practices aid and abet what anthropologists such as Ernest Becker refer to as the "denial of death." Whereas in traditional societies death and dying are regularly witnessed, in industrialized countries the aging and dying processes, with their frustrations and pains, are carefully hidden from view. Most often, old and sick people spend their final days in retirement or assisted-living institutions, and the majority of people die in the hospital, away from home and their loved ones. Corpses are shuffled to morgues and funeral homes, to be prepared for burial by professional embalmers and "funeral directors"; cosmetics are applied to make the dead appear as "natural" as possible; cremation with sanitary urns of ashes is preferred to the messy internment of decomposing bodies; memorial services are held in lieu of funeral rites; and lengthy mourning is discouraged. In sum, death has now become a taboo subject and is safely tucked away from society, invisible and unthreatening, at best an inconvenience for the living, at worst an interruption of our frantic endeavor to secure our "unalienable rights" such as "Life, Liberty and the Pursuit of Happiness."

It was not so in the late Middle Ages. As life was "solitary, poor, nasty, brutish and short," as Thomas Hobbes puts it, death was ever lurking around the corner. There was then the allegory of the Dance of Death or *danse macabre*, in which people of all walks of life, along with a pope and an emperor, are represented as dancing toward the grave, a grim reminder of the fragility of life and the inevitability of death. In 1415, some 60 years after the Black Death, which killed an estimated 25 million people in Europe, a text was composed by a Dominican friar entitled *Tractatus* (or *Speculum*) *artis bene moriendi* [Treatise on the Art of Dying Well] as a guide for a holy death. The author describes the five temptations that especially beset the dying, namely, lack of faith, despair, impatience, pride, and avarice, and shows how they can be overcome by imitating Christ and trusting in his love. Today, the inevitability of death and the necessity of a spiritual preparation are brought out vividly on Ash Wednesday, when the faithful are signed with ashes and are urged to remember that *they* (and not someone else or people in general!) shall die: "Thou art dust and unto dust thou shalt return" (*memento mori*). And the black sign of the cross traced with ashes on the forehead reminds those who happen to see it that they too will die. Through this liturgy and through countless other occasions scattered throughout life such as a serious accident, a debilitating illness, the daily pains of old age, or the death of a loved one, each of us is brought face to face with his or her own mortality. We may choose to ignore the footsteps of approaching death or we may consciously and personally listen to its insistent whisper. The difference may be between the Peter Pan (not: Peter Phan) Syndrome and the beginning of wisdom.

In the last chapter I have pointed out that the huge amount of scientific information that is now available on dying as a physiological act does not make the *meaning* of death any clearer. To understand this mysterious reality we need another source of knowledge, namely, divine revelation and religion. Before expounding what Christian faith has to say about death and dying, I would like to make a few remarks on the essential ambiguity of this phenomenon. First, we must resist the exclusively medical concept of death as an irreversible and permanent cessation of certain vital bodily functions such as respiration, heart beat, electrical activities of the brain, the presence of which can be established through procedures such as electrocardiography (EKG) and electroencephalography (EEG). While the absence of these functions must be established to declare a clinical death, it cannot be used as the only criterion to understand what death is, even from a purely medical point of view. The reason is that since death is the cessation of life, we must first understand what human life is in order to understand what death is, and such understanding is not yet available.

This brings us to the second point, namely that, even on the biological level, human life is a continuum of vital activities sustained by an ongoing process of coming-to-be and ceasing-to-be. Indeed, the very coming-to-be of one part of our bodily organism is made possible by the ceasing-to-be of another part. There is a continual process of birth-death-birth of cells in our bodies so that life may be sustained; it begins at the very moment of conception and is carried forward continuously until it is exhausted. In this view there is no clear-cut demarcation line between life and death, and though for legal purposes the moment of death must be determined and declared (legal death), we must not fixate ourselves on the precise moment when clinical death occurs, as though, when a person is declared "dead" at 5:49 AM, we could say with certainty that he or she had been "alive" before that moment in time, and after that, "deceased."

Third, this view of life as an ebb-and-flow, upward-and-downward movement, which is espoused by the Chinese religious tradition called Daoism, questions the rationale for the so-called "death with dignity" argument for euthanasia. Behind this argument lies the view that between life and death there is an absolute dividing point, medically determinable, and it is in the power of the sick person and/or the physician to end or prolong life before and beyond that point at will. Of course, the two forms of non-free euthanasia, namely, involuntary (coerced) and non-voluntary (without the conscious and informed consent of the person concerned) are unquestionably immoral since both amount to murder. But even voluntary euthanasia, that is, *freely and actively* terminating life by oneself (suicide) or through another agent with the person's free and informed consent ("assisted suicide" and "mercy killing") is also morally questionable. Beside theological reasons such as that human life is God's gift entrusted to our care and that only God has the power to bestow or remove it, there is also the fact that life and death, as pointed out above, are so inextricably intertwined that it is impossible to know the precise point at which it is proper to actively end life and begin another phase of existence.

This does not of course imply that a person must prolong life at all costs and by all possible means. This brings to my fourth point, namely, that human life is to be seen as life-in-community, in interdependence with other human beings and with the world itself. To exist is to co-exist in mutual relations in a community. In order to be able to live at all, we depend on others, just as others depend on us, in a web of mutual assistance. When for a variety of reasons living has become permanently and irreversibly impossible without a continuous assistance of others and medical support, and when one's continued living has become an unbearable physical and financial burden for oneself and/or others, and when oneself has become incapable of contributing to the welfare of others, it is reasonable and morally acceptable to conclude that one's life has run its course. At this point, it is morally legitimate to refuse medical procedures to prolong life that are, in the words of *Catechism of the Catholic Church*, "burdensome, dangerous, extraordinary, or disproportionate to the expected outcome" (§2278). The decision to refuse treatment, referred to as *passive euthanasia*, may be made only by the patient, and if incompetent, by those legally entitled to act for the patient. At the same time, all possible palliative measures must be taken, including drugs, to reduce as much as possible pains, even at the risk of shortening the patient's life.

Death: A Natural End or a Punishment for Sin?

It is interesting to note that the above-mentioned issues regarding a person's decision about death—the medical, legal, political, and ethical aspects of which provoke fierce debates today—did not concern the ancient people of the Bible. Part of the reason is that it is only thanks to the advances of modern medicine that the means of prolonging, and alternatively, terminating the patient's life have become widely available, and their use prompts vigorous debates in a new discipline called medical ethics. Furthermore, in contrast to the medical view, which tends to regard death as a defeat for science, the Bible regards death and dying in a certain respect as a natural process of living. Psalm 90 puts it with clear-eyed realism:

> *The days of our life are seventy years,*
> *or perhaps eighty, if we are strong,*
> *even then their span is only toil and trouble;*
> *they are soon gone, and we fly away (Ps 90:10).*

Death is not something to be feared, especially if it comes at the end of a life blessed with longevity, wealth, and progeny. For the Bible, what is terrifying about death is not termination of life, which is seen as a biological necessity, but the loss of fellowship with God. The dead, both righteous and unrighteous, all descend into *Sheol* (*Hades* in Greek; English translation: hell), dwell in this place of darkness as "shades," and are cut off from God. Again, as the author of Psalm 88 cries out to God:

> *For my soul is full of troubles,*
> *and my life draws near to Sheol.*
> *I am counted among those who go down to the Pit....*
> *Like those whom you remember no more,*
> *for they are cut off from your hand (vv. 3-5).*

In contrast to this naturalistic view of death, there is another, theological in perspective, that sees death as a punishment for sin. The opening pages of the Bible begin with the creation of the world as a good thing by God, and then follow up with the story of humanity's lack of trust in God and disobedience to God's command not to eat of the tree of the knowledge of good and evil under the penalty of death (Gen 2:17). Whether the first parents were created immortal or not, the Bible does not explicitly say, but it is clear that death is now a punishment for sin. God said to Adam after his transgression:

> By the sweat of your face
> you shall eat bread
> until you return to the ground,
> for out of it you were taken;
> you are dust,
> and to dust you shall return (Gen 3:19).

This view of death as punishment for sin is reiterated by Paul: "Just as sin came into the world through one man, and death came through sin, and so death spread to all because all have sin" (Rom 5:12). Later, in the same letter he says laconically: "The wages of sin is death" (Rom 6:23).

It must be pointed out at once that, in contrast to our contemporary concerns, the perspective of the Bible, and of Paul in particular, is not biological. Their interest is not in the physiological aspects of death, and whether death as termination of life is the punishment for sin (one may think that it is not), but in death as a symbol and result of our opposition to and separation from God, the Author of life (Acts 3:15). As Paul says: "To set the mind on the flesh is death" (Rom 8:6), flesh (sarx) standing for all that is opposed to God. The First Letter of John distinguishes between "sin that is mortal" and "sin that is not mortal" (5:16-17). It goes on to say: "Whoever does not love abides in death" (3:14). The Book of Revelation speaks of "the second death" (2:11; see also Jude 12), that is, eternal perdition. It is this "spiritual death," of which the physical death is a symbol, that concerns the Bible. The biblical view of sin is theological, and more precisely, soteriological, that is, having to do with our salvation. The Bible only concerns with death as a reality connected with sin, redemption, and resurrection. It is an interesting feature of the New Testament that the word nekros [dead] occurs most of the times in connection with the resurrection from the dead. Death as such is dealt with only tangentially and indirectly, as something from which Christ has saved us through his own death and resurrection.

Dying In and With Christ

It is one of the paradoxes of the Christian faith that death is vanquished only by death; more precisely, by the most shameful of deaths, that is, the death of the innocent Jesus on the cross. This is the leitmotif of the New Testament, especially the letters of Paul. Of course, the central theme is Jesus' resurrection and glorification, but his death is the means for and the doorway to life. It is a deep conviction of the Christian faith that through his death Christ has destroyed sin, and hence its consequence, death. Of course, as long as history lasts, Christians still die the physical death, but because of Christ's death, death has been robbed of its sting, like a snake that can still bite but has lost its poison. Paul asserts that "Christ, having been raised from the dead, will never die again; death no longer has dominion over him" (Rom 6:9). Triumphantly, Paul writes: "Death has been swallowed up in victory" in Christ's death and resurrection and taunts: "Where, O death, is your sting?" (1 Cor 15:55).

For Paul, those who have been baptized have been baptized into Christ's death and "have been buried with him into death, so that, just as Christ was raised from the dead by the glory of the Father, so we too might walk in newness of life" (Rom 6:4). Christians have been freed from a triple bondage, that is, to law, sin, and death (Rom 8:2). Physical death can no longer separate us from the love of God in Christ Jesus (Rom 8:38-39).

Dying a Holy Death

That in baptism Christians have died with Christ, have been buried into his death, and have been, like Jesus, raised to new life, does not at all mean that they are free from the fear and pains of death, much less that they should not daily prepare for it. In times of war (with the threat of nuclear annihilation) and pandemic (such as the Black Death or AIDS or the threat of Ebola), when life is under severe threat, thoughts of death impinge upon our consciousness and fill us with dread, but quickly subside when things turn for the better. Today, our society is in the denial-of-death mood, banishing death from its midst, and our defense mechanism reinforces such an attitude.

Perhaps today more than ever we need a new *ars moriendi*, of course not the kind of the late Middle Ages that aims at terrifying the dying into making a death-bed conversion so as to avoid eternal hell, but one that speaks meaningfully to us, citizens of the modern world who have at a click of the mouse a vast reservoir of information on the physiology and psychology of dying at our disposal, and possess the means to prolong or terminate our lives at will. Woodcuts of bands of devils with horns, red eyes, fangs, hooves, and tails encircling our death beds, ready to snatch our souls to drag them into hell, no longer terrify most of us. Nor do the images of the Day of Last Judgment evoked by the Latin sequence *Dies Irae* [Day of Wrath], which used to be sung at the Requiem Mass (now known as Mass for Christian Burial), make us cower in fear.

What we now need is an "art of dying well" that helps us face our mortality honestly and soberly, and above all, promotes "holy living." The first task in learning to die well is facing our own death squarely and honestly. The temptation to use all kinds of coping mechanisms to avoid looking at my own death face to face is well-nigh irresistible. But the price of this death-denial is unacceptably high. Unless we own our mortality, as philosophers such as Søren Kierkegaard and Martin Heidegger have argued, unless, as Heidegger puts it, we appropriate our "being-toward-death" as our "ownmost possibility," acknowledging that *I* shall die, we cannot live an authentically human life. Humans die more of a death than animals, and part of the difference lies in our awareness of our mortality. We can of course suppress this awareness by banishing all thoughts about it, or by distracting ourselves with a multitude of frenetic and banal activities, or by defiantly refusing to go gently into that good night, all this of course to no avail and in utter futility, and we will miss the unique opportunity to prepare ourselves in genuine freedom for our act of dying and our final destiny.

Furthermore, from the Christian point of view, accepting one's own mortality is an act of true humility, recognizing oneself as a created and finite being and thus ontologically different from God who alone is immortal and eternal. Paradoxically, owning our own mortality helps us overcome death anxiety (the morbid and persistent fear of death), or worse, necrophobia (irrational fear of dead things) and thanatophobia (fear of dying or being dead), all of which produce a mental paralysis and prevent us from living a full life.

This acknowledgment of mortality must also be sober, that is, free from exaggeration and morbidity. It should not lead to cynicism and despair, believing that nothing is worth doing, or doing well, since death will be the end of it all. Nor should death be romanticized and stripped of all its horrors. Not all will be able to praise God for "Sister Death," as Saint Francis of Assisi did, or welcome it as a "friend," as the Dutch priest and pastoral theologian Henri Nouwen counsels. These attitudes toward death remain the ideals to which we, run-of-the-mill people, aspire but may never reach. Meanwhile, the least we can do is to come to an ever-fuller realization of the inevitability and nearness of our death, though ordinarily we do not know its exact timing. This awareness needs not lead to sadness and depression. On the contrary, it will allow us to make the most out of every day and moment, living it to the fullest.

Finally, the new *ars moriendi* [the art of dying] must lead to a new *ars vivendi* [the art of living], that is, a new way of living well. Though death bed conversions are not impossible, normally one dies the kind of death one prepares for during one's life. In his helpful book *The Art of Dying and Living*, Kerry Walters describes seven interconnected virtues or "habits of the hearts" for dying well as they are exemplified by seven Christians, namely, trust, love, gratitude, obedience, courage, patience, and discernment of God's presence in one's whole life ("christing," to use Caryll Houselander's expression). These virtues are not simply habits for dying a holy death; they are ways of living well that lead to a holy death. Of course, it is not enough to read about these habits of the heart; one rarely if ever becomes virtuous by reading about virtues, just as one does not become drunk by reading about wines. More effective than reading books and listening to lectures about dying is witnessing first-hand how saints have died. For instance, well-known to American Catholics are Cardinal Joseph Bernardin, Sister Theo Bowman, and Saint John Paul II, whose deaths have been movingly narrated by Kerry Walters. Of course, we don't need to look at popes, bishops and Religious to find people who have died holy deaths. Often they are members of our families, our grandparents and parents, our husbands and wives and children, and our friends. The greatest gift they have given us is their art of living well and dying well.

Of all religions perhaps Tibetan Buddhism offers the most detailed guide to dying well. Its funerary text, popularly known as the *Tibetan Book of the Dead* (*bardo thodol*; the full title is: *Liberation Through Hearing During the Intermediate State*), is recited by the lamas over the dying or the recently deceased to guide him or her through the different intermediate stages of existence between death and rebirth to achieve liberation. There is no need to accept all the Buddhist teachings of this book to appreciate the extreme importance of "letting-go" of all desires, what the Buddha calls "desire" or "greed" (*tanha*), which is said to be the root of all sufferings, to live well and to die well.

The above-mentioned writer Kerry Walters speaks of three movements required for holy living and holy dying: letting-go, letting-be, and cleaving to God. All three actions form the virtue of trust or faith. For Christians, letting-go consists in giving up one's need to be in control of one's life; letting-be is accepting one's death as the natural end of one's life and allowing God to be God; and cleaving-to-God is trusting that God will receive one's life into God's life.

Accompanying the Dying: We Will Not Die Alone

Often we envy those who die after a long life but without experiencing the debilitating and humiliating effects of old age and illness. Of course, we may pray for such a blessing. But there are perhaps spiritual advantages to old age and terminal illnesses. It is psychologically difficult to think of mortality in the midst of youth and vigor. But when eyesight gets dimmer, hearing harder, steps faltering, when merely getting out of bed for another day is a physical ordeal, when we depend on others to perform the simplest of bodily functions, and especially when we are told that our days are numbered, it is difficult—and foolish—to ignore death's knocks on our door. We are thus given the grace—and the time—to learn to let go, let be, and cleave to God, in patience and trust. In the waning days of our life, we can lament in despair, as Jesus did on the cross: "My God, my God, why have you forsaken me?" (Mk 15:14) and at the same time, utter with trust, again as Jesus did: "Father, into your hands I commend my spirit" (Lk 23:46). In the face of death, we sinners must pray for this overcoming of despair with trust, "now and at the hour of our death," as the "Hail Mary" beautifully ends.

Of course, such peaceful and "good" death is a blessing we should all pray for. But it is not a passive prayer; there are some things we can and must do to help the terminally ill persons go through the dying process with dignity and peace. One of the most helpful developments in recent times is the hospice movement. Hospice aims at providing patients having a life expectancy of six months or less and their loved ones with physical, emotional, and spiritual comfort. Its goal is neither to prolong life nor to hasten death. Depending on the physical condition of the patient and availability of means, hospice can take place at the patient's home, in an assisted living or nursing home, or in a hospice facility. Hospice as end-of-life care provides the living with the opportunity to accompany the dying with comforting presence, loving care, and prayerful support. It is perhaps the most needed "work of mercy" that we can do for the dying in our contemporary society where a majority of patients die in the hospital in isolation, alone, bereft of the comforting presence and support of their loved ones.

The Catholic Church, carrying out Jesus' command: "Heal the sick" (Mt 10:8), not only has a special ministry for the sick and the elderly but also celebrates the sacrament of the Anointing of the Sick. Formerly known as the "Extreme Unction" because it was given only to those on the point of death, today this sacrament, as indicated by its new name, is administered to those in danger of death because of serious sickness, life-threatening surgery, and old age. Ideally it should be celebrated with the community, preceded by the sacrament of penance (reconciliation or confession) and within the Mass. With blessed oil, the priest anoints the sick on the forehead and hands, and says: "Through this holy anointing may the Lord in his love and mercy help you with the grace of the Holy Spirit. May the Lord who frees you from sin save you and raise you up." The grace of the Holy Spirit invoked here refers to the healing of the sick, not only in the soul but also in the body, if this is God's will. The sacrament also unites the sick with the passion and death of Jesus, making them more "configured" to Jesus in their suffering. In this way the sick contribute to the holiness of the church. Finally, the sacrament of Anointing of the Sick prepares the sick for their final journey to the Father's home. In addition to the sacrament of anointing, to those on the point of death, the church offers the body and blood of Christ as food for the journey (*viaticum*), as the seed of the resurrection and eternal life, as Jesus has promised: "He who eats my flesh and drinks my blood has eternal life, and I will raise him up at the last day" (Jn 6:54).

But the church's presence with the dead does not end there; it accompanies them to the very end. The Christian community gathers to say farewell to the deceased, mourn their passing, and comfort their surviving family. The celebration of Christian funerals may begin in the home of the deceased, continues with the Eucharist in the church, and concludes with the burial at the cemetery, or to use the quaintly comforting term, 'churchyard.' In this final moment, when death is both *end* and *beginning*, when death that is punishment for sin is transformed into an act of total self-surrender in

◘ 27

faith, hope and love for God, the congregation sings the song of farewell, with the hope of reunion with the deceased in God's kingdom, and prays:

> *May the angels lead you into paradise;*
> *may the martyrs come to welcome you*
> *and take you to the holy city,*
> *the new and eternal Jerusalem.*

Angels and martyrs, indeed, in whose company our beloved dead will dwell, in the all-embracing arms of the all-merciful, all-loving, all-beautiful Triune God: Father, Son, and Spirit.

3

THE AFTERLIFE

IMMORTALITY OF THE SOUL OR ETERNAL LIFE?

Most, though not all, religions teach that there remains something of the human person in the so-called "afterlife." There seems to be a universal desire that whatever good we have achieved in our lives—even our entire "selves"—will survive after our death. Similarly, we also hope that the evil we have done will be erased, or at least its bad impact neutralized. Because not all the consequences of our actions—good and bad—can be reaped as reward or punishment in one lifetime, however long, we naturally think of the possibility of perhaps one or several more lives after this life in which to complete our task of achieving a full human flourishing, or if this possibility of reincarnation is not available and our present life is the only one given to us, then at least in the afterlife.

The English word "afterlife" does not of course tell us much about what the life hereafter will look like, except to indicate that it follows this life chronologically ("after"). The Bible however does not use expressions equivalent to the English word with its temporal connotation. Indeed, the Old Testament is not too concerned about what will come after this life except in its later books in the second century before Christ such as the Maccabees, where the vision of the resurrection of the dead and the life after death began to take shape. In contrast, the New Testament is centered on the resurrection of Christ and the kind of transformed life it brings to all humanity. To describe this kind of life the New Testament never calls it the "afterlife." It is not seen as a life that begins *after* this life and in some way continues and perpetuates it without any transformation. Rather it is called "eternal life" (*aiōnios zoē*), which already occurs here and now, especially through the life in and with Christ and by the power of the Holy Spirit. It is already actualized in the celebration of the sacraments, particularly baptism and the Eucharist, in contrast to the earthly life (*psychē*), which is destined to death.

Of course, belief in the afterlife, though well-nigh universal among religious people, is being severely challenged by our contemporary mind-set which is inclined to reject anything that cannot be scientifically tested and verified. On the other hand, a small number of scientists and psychologists have pointed out that the so-called near-death experiences that have been widely reported and well documented provide solid evidence for the reality of life after death. In addition to scientists a good number of philosophers also argue against the existence of the afterlife. Furthermore, even those who defend it do not speak of it as "eternal life" or the "resurrection of the dead" but as the "immortality of the soul." In contrast, Christians profess in the Nicene-Constantinopolitan Creed: "We expect the resurrection of the dead and the life of the world to come" and in the Apostles' Creed: "I believe in the resurrection of the body and the life everlasting."

In this chapter I first explain what is meant by "eternity." Next I examine some evidences for the possibility of the afterlife, with reference to the near-death experiences. Lastly, I examine the concept of the immortality of the soul and contrast it with the Christian notion of "eternal life."

Time and Eternity

As mentioned above, the English term "afterlife" implies temporal succession. Normally however what is stressed is not continuity but opposition between this life and what comes after it. Since we do not (yet) have experiences of the afterlife, and given the contrast between it and this life, we tend to speak of the afterlife in terms of what is opposed to what we experience in this present life. One fundamental aspect of our experience of this life is time. We all know what time is, but, as St. Augustine notes, we would be at a loss if asked to define it. It comes as no surprise that scientists, philosophers, psychologists and theologians are deeply interested in understanding the nature of time. The starting point is our experience of movement, and time is the measurement of the movement from the past through the present into the future. It is *chronological* time, the kind of time indicated by the clock in terms of second, minute and hour. It is characterized by movement and irreversibility, like the sands flowing from the upper half of an hourglass down to its lower half—the past is gone, the present is transitory, and the future is yet to come, in an irreversible direction. Physicists speak of time as the fourth dimension of the universe, in addition to the three dimensions of space (each dimension constituted by a combination of three chosen from length, width, depth, and breath), and try to determine the beginning moment of time.

Some philosophers such as the German Immanuel Kant argue that time is not something real, an independent dimension of the universe, a sort of container in which events occur and flow sequentially, as Isaac Newton thinks, but is only a conceptual scheme (along with space and number) with which the human mind structures its experience of the world. For instance, when speaking of something I have done, I have to locate it somewhere and sometime. Psychologists speak of "narrative time"—time that is not measured on the geologic time scale, but by a person's "internal clock" formed by various mental states. For instance, reading this chapter may seem an eternity in hell if you find it boring to death, or time seems to fly if you are having fun with it. For Christian theologians time itself is created by God. God, as Augustine has noted, creates the universe *with* time, not *in* time, since there was no time before creation. Being-in-time then is an index of creaturehood and finiteness.

In light of these various understandings of time (chronological time and psychological time), life after death is said to be the opposite, or at least absence of time, or "timelessness," or "eternity." In using these words to refer to the afterlife, we must take care to avoid a common error. Induced by misleading phrases such as "forever and ever " (the common translation of the sonorous Latin phrase: *per saecula saeculorum*), "world without end," or "everlasting," we tend to imagine eternal life as a chronological, linear movement running on and on and on, without ever coming to a stop, as popularly represented by the image of Father Time handing over the time-keeping duties to Baby New Year, or by the *ourobouros*, the ancient symbol depicting a serpent swallowing its own tail. Rather than endless time, that is time without end, eternity is *timelessness*, that is life without time at all, that is, without the movement or change from the past through the present to the future. It is the enjoyment of the simultaneity of the whole and perfect life.

The sixth-century Roman philosopher Boethius (ca. 480-524/5) defines eternity as "the simultaneous, whole and perfect possession of interminable life" (*aeternitas est interminabilis vitae tota simul et perfecta possessio*). In this sense, eternity is not simply this life made endless, but the termination of this life as we know it, with all its imperfections and limitations, or better still, *transformation* of it into something like God's life; indeed it is a total and perfect *participation* in God's life. I will have opportunities to explain in greater detail what Christian faith says about eternal life, especially as it is given by Christ. Christian faith has much more to say, vastly more enriching and profound, than what science, psychology and philosophy can say about eternity and what humans can hope to possess. For now it is sufficient to note that eternal life is not just a continuation and perpetuation of this life in some other, better place than this world, as might be suggested by the popular phrase often used after a person's death, especially if it is preceded by a long, painful illness: "He/she is in a better place now." Rather it is a total, simultaneous, and perfect possession of the life of God. What this eternal life is, Christian tradition has much to say, as we will see later when we speak of heaven in chapter 6.

Near-Death Experiences and Eternal Life

Before we go on to speak about the afterlife and the immortality of the soul, there is a preliminary question that begs for an answer: Is there any proof that such a life exists? With the publication of Raymond Moody's book *Life After Life* (1975) and the works of Dr. Elisabeth Kübler Ross, widespread interest was aroused in what is called "near-death experiences" (NDE). People who had been almost dead or declared clinically dead have revived, and with new techniques of cardiac resuscitation, the number of these cases has increased exponentially. As recently as 1992, some eight million Americans reported to have had a NDE. A variety of phenomena are claimed to occur in NDE, including out-of-body experiences, entering a dark tunnel, seeing beings of light, life review, a deep sense of peace, and awareness of returning to life. Study of NDE has become a booming cottage industry with its own associations, journals, and research centers, and involves different academic fields such as psychology, psychiatry, hospital medicine, and theology

Do these NDE prove that there is life after death? A straightforward answer is unfortunately not forthcoming, and it varies according to the field in which research is done. In general, scientists and psychologists tend to emphasize a naturalistic and neurological base for NDE, while some medical doctors (e.g., Jeffrey Long) claim that these experiences cannot adequately be accounted for by merely physiological and psychological causes and demonstrate that human consciousness can function independently of brain activities (Jeffrey Long, M.D. with Paul Perry, *Evidence of the Afterlife: The Science of Near-Death Experiences* [New York: HarperCollins, 2011]). In contrast, several theologians such as Terence Nichols see in NDE evidence confirming the Christian belief in the existence of the soul, the afterlife, and even the existence of heaven and hell (Terence Nichols, *Death and Afterlife: A Theological Introduction* [Grand Rapids, MI: Brazos Press, 2010]).

Clearly, for those who already believe that there is the afterlife, NDE provide a welcome confirmation for their belief. On the other hand, those who think that the so-called "mind" is nothing but brain and those who are philosophically opposed to the notion of immortality and the soul tend to dismiss accounts of NDE as nothing more than psychological or cultural expressions of the wish for survival beyond the grave.

In my judgment, NDE are not apodictic proofs for the existence of the afterlife or of the immortality of the soul. At best they show that there are cases in which some conscious activity after the "clinical death" is possible, at least for a brief period of time (after all, they are *near*-death and not *after*-death experiences), and even if these experiences cannot be explained away in purely physiological, chemical, psychological, and cultural terms, it is highly doubtful that these transitory and momentary post-clinical death conscious activities can be identified as "afterlife" or "soul" as these realities are commonly understood.

Nevertheless, near-death experiences are suggestive pointers to, or at the very least raise intriguing and provocative questions about the *possibility* of the afterlife. Furthermore, it is to be noted that the issues of the existence of the soul and the afterlife are beyond the field of competence of scientists and medical doctors. As individuals, they may or may not believe in them, but qua scientists they can neither affirm nor deny it, and must not do so, on the basis of their academic research. At best they may say that the phenomena reported in the NDE are or are not accountable by the currently known physiological processes, but they are not entitled to go beyond this and say anything positive or negative about the possibility of the afterlife.

Finally, what is most significant about NDE is not what they may reveal about the afterlife but that those who experience them return to life with a renewed commitment to live a better life, with no feeling of moral superiority and no claim to intellectual infallibility. They bear eloquent witness to the fact that what finally matters is not what occurs at the moment of death but the kind of life one lives toward a holy death.

Immortality of the Soul or Eternal Life?

The last question to be discussed is whether death brings an end to everything in the human person. In other words, is there anything that will survive death and the dissolution of the body? Implicit in this question is the distinction within the human person between the "body" and something traditionally called the "soul." Though the meaning of the human body in the person and in society is complex and has recently been a subject of extensive debate in scholarly circles, what is referred to by "body" is, at first sight at least, obvious. We can, for example, point to our foot, and say: "This is part of my body," and safely assume that everybody understands what we mean. No such thing of course can be taken for granted with regard to the soul. We cannot point to anything in us and say: "This is my soul."

But what is 'soul'? The primary dictionary definition of 'soul' is: "the immaterial essence, animating principle, actuating cause of an individual life," or "the spiritual principle embodied in human beings, all rational and spiritual beings, or the universe" (*Webster's New Collegiate Dictionary*). It is taken to be opposite to, or at least distinct from, the 'body'; and in contrast to the body which is mortal, the soul is said to be immaterial, spiritual, and immortal.

As with the meaning of human bodiliness, the immortality of the soul has been intensively debated throughout the history of philosophy and recently in science. Furthermore, in theology, it has been questioned whether the immortality of the soul, even if it can be philosophically grounded, is what Christian faith means by 'eternal life.' Among ancient Greek philosophers, the most noted defender of the immortality of the soul is no doubt Plato. Inherent in Plato's argument is a dualism between body and soul. The soul, which pre-exists the body, is condemned to dwell in the mortal body as in a prison, and its goal is to be liberated from it and retrieve its immortality. For Aristotle, the soul is the "energy" of life animating the body. Rejecting Plato's dualism, he maintains that the body and the soul constitute a single "substance" of the human person. He does not however believe that the soul of each person is immortal; but only the universal, active soul, in which each human soul participates, is.

In general, however, most Western philosophers hold that the soul, being spiritual and immaterial, survives death and that this truth can be rationally demonstrated. In contrast, the eighteenth-century German philosopher Immanuel Kant argues that since our knowledge is limited only to empirical things, the immortality of the soul cannot be rationally proved by the "pure reason" but must be postulated by the "practical reason" for the sake of morality. The immortality of the soul is one of the three "postulates" for ethics, the other two being the existence of God and human freedom. Without presupposing these three realities, Kant argues, it would be impossible to justify why we must behave ethically. Along the same lines, many modern scientists hold that it is meaningless to speak of 'soul'; we can only speak of 'brain,' or at best 'mind,' and that its functions, which are totally dependent on the body, will cease with death.

A contemporary British philosopher Stephen Cave argues that humans have an innate desire to live forever and attempt to achieve it along one, or a combination of some or all, of the following four paths: science and technology (through cryonics, for instance), the resurrection of the body, the immortality of the soul, and leaving behind a permanent legacy. According to Cave, these four ways seek to resolve what he calls the "mortality paradox," that is, our awareness of our own mortality and our inability to conceive our death to ourselves (Stephen Cave, *Immortality: The*

Quest to Live Forever and How It Drives Civilization [New York, Crown Publishers, 2011]).

As mentioned earlier, to uphold the immortality of the soul logically presupposes a real distinction and separability between the body and the soul. *Catechism of the Catholic Church*, which teaches the immortality of the soul, makes this connection clear: "The Church teaches that every spiritual soul is created immediately by God—it is not 'produced' by the parents—and also that it is immortal: it does not perish when it separates from the body at death, and it will be reunited with the body at the final Resurrection" (§366).

We will come back to this body-soul distinction in chapter 5 and its implications for understanding the so-called intermediate state between death and the general resurrection, especially with regard to the "separated soul" (*anima separata*). Here I would like to make the following four points: First, the belief in the existence of the first humans Adam and Eve living in the garden of Eden does not in itself require the belief that Adam and Eve would not die. Death as simple termination of life, the final effect of entropy, may be a natural and unavoidable consequence of having a body. Only as an event of final separation from God and from one's fellow human beings, that is, as a *human*, and not just physiological act, is death a consequence of sin. Thus, even if one's first parents had not sinned, they and their descendants would still "die" in the sense that their biological life will come to a natural end.

Second, the belief in the resurrection does not entail the belief that immortality is a natural, innate attribute of the soul. It may be taken to be an additional gift of God to humans. In other words, one may think that when a person dies, the whole person, that is, both the body and the soul, perish. In this case, resurrection may be understood to mean the raising to life of the entire human person, of *both* the body the soul, after their death, by a gracious act of God.

Third, we may not be able, nor is it required by the Christian faith, to prove by rational argument the immortality of the soul; rather we may accept this truth on the basis of faith. We need not subscribe to Kant's theory that the immortality of the soul is only a postulate of the practical reason for the sake of establishing ethical norms. One may simply hold that the immortality of the soul is not a truth that can be known by means of unaided reason but a truth that has been revealed by God.

Lastly, and perhaps most significantly, it must be noted that what the Bible means by the resurrection of the dead goes far beyond what philosophers mean by the immortality of the soul. No doubt, as many cultural historians have pointed out, the concept of 'soul' and its immortality has driven and shaped the entire mind-set of Western civilization. The conviction that there is a spiritual and imperishable element in the human being that can be ascertained by reason, apart from any divine revelation or belief in a divine creator, gives intrinsic and inviolable dignity to each and every human being. It is this understanding of the human person that lies at the foundation of the affirmation and defense of human rights and the promotion of democracy in secular societies.

Notwithstanding the above four observations, a careful reading of Scripture will reveal that the central focus of the Christian message is not the immortality of the soul, though this is not excluded, but eternal life. What this reality is will be discussed in the various chapters of this book when we speak of the resurrection of the dead, heaven, the transformation of the world, the Eucharist, and the kingdom of God. Here I would like to use a "parable" proposed by one of the great Australian theologians, Anthony Kelly. Kelly argues that eternal life is rooted in the life, death, and resurrection of Jesus which is, in Kelly's memorable phrase, the "parable of hope" (Anthony Kelly, *Eschatology and Hope* [Maryknoll, NY: Orbis Books, 2006]). This parable of hope is rooted in turn in the reality of the eternal love that constitutes God as Father, Son, and Spirit. This love is trinitarian: God the Father is the origin of this eternal love; God the Son is this love as given; God the Spirit is this love as communicated. Eternal life is nothing less than the consummation of this love in human persons, societies, and the cosmos.

Clearly, eternal life is vastly more than the endless continuation of this present life, or the survival of the spiritual element after our death. It is our complete and perfect communion with the Trinitarian God, all other human beings that have ever existed, and the cosmos. As we will see in later chapters, religious imagination describes it in richly evocative images and symbols, as Dante has done in his *Divina Commedia*. Sometimes our imagination runs wild, and heaven looks like the consumerist's well-stocked shopping mall or the holiday-maker's ideal vacation spot. This picture of heaven will do no harm as long as we remember that it is just what it is, an *image*, and not the reality itself. Furthermore, this reality is not something that will only come *after* this life (the *after*-life). It is already a reality in this world, albeit in imperfect form. Additionally, it must be made real and witnessed to ("sacramentalized") by the community of the disciples of Jesus called church, as they, in collaboration with the believers of other religions, and indeed, with all humans, including people without religious faith, work together to make a world of justice, peace, and the integrity of creation. Thus, Christian belief in eternal life is not, and must not be used as, an opium for the oppressed mass but is an incentive to bring about a world in which all persons, and the cosmos itself, can achieve full flourishing, in which *both* the corruptible body and the immortal soul of each and every human person will find perfect fulfillment.

4

THE REIGN OF GOD AS THE GOAL OF HISTORY

WHAT DID JESUS LIVE AND DIE FOR?

If you are interested in finding out what Jesus thinks about death and the afterlife, especially his view about when the world will end and what hell and heaven look like, you will be sorely disappointed. The gospels report precious little about what Jesus believed and said about these things. Of course Jesus did talk about them, but quite rarely, and always in parables or in a roundabout way that would greatly frustrate those seeking detailed and exact information. On the one hand, we can safely assume that as a Jew, Jesus professes the Jewish beliefs about life after death. In particular, Jesus sides with the Pharisees against the Sadducees in affirming the resurrection of the body "on the last day." On the other hand, when directly challenged by the Sadducees on this belief with the trick question about the woman with seven husbands, Jesus simply says that people after the resurrection from the dead "neither marry nor are given in marriage. Indeed they cannot die anymore, because they are equal to angels and are children of God,

◘ 41

being children of the resurrection" (Lk 20:35-36). Had I been present at the debate between Jesus and the Sadducees, I would certainly have asked Jesus about the time of the resurrection, the kind of bodies the "children of the resurrection" will have, what kinds of fun things they can do with their bodies if they "neither marry nor are given in marriage," whether there will be enough room on earth for trillions upon trillions of people, and a host of other issues. But I doubt that Jesus would give my questions the time of day, because the overwhelming concern of his life is not to satisfy our curiosity about things in the afterlife but about something else.

What is this "something else" about which Jesus was really concerned? The short answer is: the kingdom, or reign, of God. It is not that the kingdom of God has nothing to do with eternal life. Indeed, it has everything to do with it. But it is only within the context of Jesus' teaching on and ministry in the service of the kingdom of God that we can understand his message about death and eternal life. I begin with the teaching of Jesus on the kingdom of God, with particular reference to the apocalyptic movement during his time. Next I present the teaching of Paul and the gospels on eschatology. Lastly I reflect on the death of Jesus as the model for our dying since what Jesus lived and died for should also be what we live and die for.

Jesus as the Reign of God

If there is a single verse in the New Testament that encapsulates Jesus' teaching and ministry, it is Mk 1:14: "The time is fulfilled, and the kingdom of God has come near; repent, and believe in the good news." What is the kingdom that Jesus proclaims as having come near and as good news? The answer to this question requires knowledge of the context of Jesus' proclamation which in biblical circles is referred to as "apocalyptic."

First of all, Jesus stands in the tradition of the Hebrew prophets whose task is to discern and interpret God's will for their contemporaries, and not to predict the future, as the word 'prophecy' in English might suggest. Because their situation is marked by widespread transgressions against God's covenant, the ancient prophets regularly threaten the people with divine punishments in terms of natural disasters, loss of monarchy and priesthood, exile from the land, desecration of the Temple, profanation of the cult of Yahweh, and sufferings of all kinds.

However, God's punishments are not intended to destroy the people but to convert them back to God and bring them salvation. Virtually all the prophets who were active during and after the exile in 587 BC announce the imminent coming of a new age in which God will deliver God's people. This promised salvation would be brought about either directly by God or through an intermediary, variously named the Suffering Servant or the Messiah. This new age is called "the kingdom/reign/rule of God," in which God rules over not only Israel but also all the nations and the cosmos in truth, justice, and peace.

Unfortunately the ideal and at times idyllic description of the eschatological age that is given by the prophets far outstrips reality. Bitter disappointments poisoned the wellspring of hope when the spiritual condition of the people did not improve after their return from exile to their homeland and the restoration of Temple, cult, and priesthood. Hope was not given up, however, even after the loss of national independence, first to the Greeks, and then to the Romans. On the contrary, a new movement, known in biblical studies circle as "apocalyptic" (from the Greek *apocalypsis*, meaning unveiling or revelation), with its corresponding literature, soon emerged. Apocalyptic espouses not the restoration of this present evil age but its *destruction* and the creation of a *new age*. In the Old Testament the prime example of apocalyptic literature is the Book of Daniel, and in the New Testament, the Book of Revelation.

This apocalyptic movement and thought was vibrant at Jesus' time, and Jesus himself is thought by the majority of scholars to stand within its circle. At the beginning of his public ministry Jesus was baptized by John the Baptizer, who, in the hallowed tradition of apocalyptic prophets, radically condemned the established order of Israel, called for national repentance to prepare for the imminent arrival of the Coming One, and indeed hailed Jesus as that Coming One. Jesus' choice of the twelve disciples has the symbolic meaning of the renewal of the twelves tribes of Israel. His cleansing of the Temple is a prophetic symbol of its destruction and renewal. His miracles are signs that the new world was aborning. And, finally, his execution by the Roman authorities for alleged sedition shows that they perceived him as one of the apocalyptic revolutionaries.

It is in this apocalyptic context that Jesus announces the imminent coming of the kingdom of God and affirms that it has already begun in his life and ministry, though of course its completion is still to come. Like any other apocalyptic prophet, Jesus does not provide the exact time of the arrival of the kingdom of God but insists on its imminence and urges constant vigilance and readiness. He does of course provide "signs" heralding the coming of God's reign, such as war, famine, fire, earthquake, and other cosmic cataclysms, as we read in the so-called eschatological discourses of Jesus in Matthew 24, Mark 13 and Luke 21. These signs are simply the stock-in-trade of the apocalyptic language quite common in Jesus' time to warn people of the magnitude of the things that will happen to them if they do not repent and believe in the good news he proclaims, a language Jesus adopts liberally. They are intended neither as a *description*, like a journalistic report, nor as a *prediction*, of the things at the end of time. Therefore, we must not try to identify these signs with this or that historical event or natural disaster to predict the coming of the end of the world, as some fundamentalist preachers have done. Indeed, Jesus himself acknowledges: "But about that day and hour no one knows, neither the angels of heaven, nor the Son, but only the Father" (Mt 24:36).

If we cannot know the time of the coming of the reign of God, at least do we know what it is? Unlike philosophers and theologians, Jesus does not define things. Rather he talks about the kingdom in parables and stories and then says: "Let anyone with ears listen!" (Mt 11:15). Different from earlier prophets and apocalypticists who emphasize the future coming of the reign of God, Jesus states that it is already present here and now, though, as I mentioned above, its final and total completion is still to come: "But if it is by the finger of God that I cast out demons, then the kingdom of God has come to you" (Lk 11:20). In other words, the kingdom of God is tied with Jesus' life and ministry.

Consequently, to understand what the kingdom of God is, we must look at not only what Jesus said but also, and especially, what he did. Now, what is utterly striking, and even scandalous, about his behavior is that Jesus welcomes into the kingdom of God those whom his society marginalizes and excludes. Comparing himself to John the Baptizer, he says: "The Son of Man came eating and drinking, and they say, 'Look, a glutton and a drunkard, a friend of tax collectors and sinners!'" (Mt 11:19). In addition to these categories, there are the economically poor, women, children, lepers, the lame and the blind, the possessed, the non-Jews, and all sorts of suffering people; in short, all those who are oppressed by the powerful simply because of their race, ethnicity, gender, social class, and physical and spiritual conditions. Liberation theologians refer to Jesus' attitude toward all these people as "the preferential option for the poor," that is, God's sharing with "the least of these" God's life, love, grace, forgiveness, peace, and all earthly blessings. That is what is meant by "eternal life." It is not something that will only come after our death, or at the end of time, in a heaven beyond this world. Rather it is already inaugurated here and now, in the person of Jesus, whom the third-century Greek theologian Origen calls the *autobasileia*—the kingdom in person. It is neither a political utopia or Shangri-la nor a purely spiritual, interior reality. Rather eternal life is *this* life, *this* world, cleansed of all evil and suffering, and transformed into the kingdom of God of justice, and peace, and integrity of creation.

Paul and The Gospels on Eternal Life

We can flesh out this understanding of eternal life as life in the kingdom of God by examining briefly what Paul and the four gospels say about it. Of course, for the early Christians, the kingdom of God that Jesus announced is realized fully by his death and resurrection.

Paul

The conviction that the kingdom of God that Jesus announced was already realized by his death and resurrection lies at the foundation of Paul's ministry. In his so-called conversion on his way to Damascus, Paul is given a revelation that God's promises to Israel have been fulfilled in the death and resurrection of Jesus of Nazareth. Being raised to life and glorified, Jesus becomes the Lord not only of Israel but of all peoples. Given Jesus' lordship over all humanity, indeed over the cosmos, salvation is no longer restricted to an ethnic or national group but becomes universal or "catholic" (with the small c). It is Paul's specific calling and ministry to share this good news to the Gentiles and to bring them to the obedience of faith.

Although Paul believes that salvation is already present in us, especially in baptism, by which we die with Christ, are buried with him, and are raised to a new life in him (Rom 8), and now live by the power of the Spirit, he never ceases to remind us that eternal life in its fullness is still to come. It will be achieved only in the resurrection of the dead when death itself, the last enemy, is destroyed and all things are subjected to Christ, and Christ to God, so that God may be all in all (1 Cor 15:28). Thus, we are now living between two aeons or ages, in the time of "already" and "not yet," by faith and not by sight, eagerly expecting in hope the full realization of salvation, or, as Paul puts it eloquently, we "who have the first fruits of the Spirit, groan inwardly while we wait for adoption, the redemption of our bodies. For in hope we were saved" (Rom 8:23-24).

Paul's vision of eternal life as our earthly life lived in the hope of eternal life helps us avoid two errors. The first is to regard salvation as liberation of the soul from the shackles of the body and return to God and heaven as its true home, as Christians with Platonic and

Gnostic tendencies tend to think. Against this spiritualistic view, Paul strongly emphasizes that eternal life includes the resurrection of the body.

What Paul thinks of the nature of the risen body will be discussed when we speak of the resurrection in chapter 8. Second, Paul's emphasis on the not-yet character of eternal life present now in us, "longing to be clothed with our heavenly dwelling" (2 Cor 5:2), prevents us from thinking that eternal life is something we can produce with our work. Rather, as Paul puts it, it is "a building from God, a house not made with hands, eternal in the heavens" (2 Cor 5:1). This truth helps us overcome disillusionment and despair when our work fails to bring about the ideal society of which we dream.

The Synoptic Gospels

Turning now to the Synoptic Gospels, I have noted above that Mark, who uses the expression the "kingdom of God" fourteen times, makes it the basic theme of Jesus' preaching. The kingdom of God, according to Mark, has come near, and demands our repentance and faith in the good news announced by Jesus. As far as eschatology is concerned, Mark 13 is the most significant text. After predicting the destruction of the Temple, Jesus gives, in typically apocalyptic imagery, a series of signs of the end-time. After a cosmic upheaval, the Son of Man will come in the clouds and gather his elect from all corners of the world.

Matthew uses the expression "kingdom of heaven" (a pious circumlocution to avoid using the word 'God') thirty-two times, "kingdom of God" four times, and "kingdom" in conjunction with other modifiers fourteen times. Evidently, the kingdom of God as eternal life is of extreme importance for Matthew. For him, in his life and ministry Jesus fulfills all the promises God makes to Israel. With regard to eschatology, chapters 24-25 are the most important, with the usual apocalyptic images. Matthew emphasizes the need for vigilance and expectation in the parable of the ten virgins and the duty of love of neighbor in the parable of the last judgment.

Luke most strongly stresses the presence of the kingdom of God in the person of Jesus: "The kingdom of God is among you" (Lk 17:21); at the same time, he notes that "the coming of the kingdom of God cannot be observed" (Lk 17:20). Luke 21 is parallel to Matthew 24-25 and Mark 13. Unlike the other two evangelists, Luke separates the destruction of the Temple and the other signs of the coming of the Son of Man by interposing an in-between period that he calls "the times of the Gentiles." In so doing Luke attempts to come to terms with the community's experience of what has been called the "delay of the Parousia," which is supposed to occur soon after the destruction of the Temple.

Of all the four gospels, John is the most strongly emphatic on the "already" of the kingdom of God. Of course, the future dimension is not forgotten: there is mention of the future resurrection "on the last day" (5:28-29; 6:39, 40, 44, 54); of Jesus' second coming (14:3, 18; 21:21-23); and of a future judgment on "the last day" (12:48). However, for the Fourth Gospel, God's eschatological judgment has already occurred in the sending of God's only Son into the world and in the human response to him. The benefits of the future salvation are already experienced in four ways: the gift of the Spirit, the possession of eternal life, the divine judgment, and the presence of Jesus as the Messiah.

The Death of Jesus, Our Model for Dying

My intent here is not to reflect on all the historical circumstances surrounding the crucifixion of Jesus and its theological meaning, especially its redemptive role in the history of salvation. My only interest is in the way Jesus died and how it can be a model for our own dying. The Swiss Protestant scholar Oscar Cullmann contrasts the way Socrates and Jesus faced their deaths.

Condemned to death by the powers-that-be of Athens for impiety and corrupting the minds of the young, Socrates welcomes his execution because, he says, it liberates his soul from the body. Calmly drinking the poisonous hemlock and reminding his friend Crito to pay his debt of a rooster to Asclepius, Socrates died peacefully and serenely.

By contrast, the Gospels tell us that Jesus was "deeply grieved, even to death" (Mk 14:34) and prayed that God, whom he called "Abba," save him from dying if that is God's will. Luke further relates that "in anguish he prayed more earnestly, and his sweat became like great drops of blood falling down on the ground" (Lk 22:43-44). (Note that some ancient manuscripts lack these two verses.) When hanging on the cross, according to Matthew and Mark, Jesus cried out in despair: "My God, my God, why have you forsaken me?" (Mt 27:46; Mk 15:34). Luke does not report this cry of Jesus, but rather says that Jesus' last words are: "Father, into your hands I commend my spirit" (Lk 23:46). John reports neither of these cries but says that Jesus' last words are: "It is finished" (Jn 19:30).

We cannot put together these three final cries of Jesus to create a harmonious account of Jesus' last words on the cross. Each evangelist has his own theological agenda in reporting this particular cry as an articulation of Jesus. We can see all three cries as expressions of three human attitudes and reactions toward death. The first expresses terror and despair, especially when death is premature, painful, and unjust. We feel we are being abandoned by not merely a divine and powerful being but by the God whom we call "Abba" (Father). We protest that we have been betrayed by the Being in whom we have entrusted our entire lives. It is the cry of despair that is uttered not only by those dying alone, abandoned, hopeless, but also by those who witness and mourn the premature and unjust death of their husband or wife, parent or child, lover or friend, whose passing leaves an unspeakable emptiness. This cry of despair and terror is a natural, not blasphemous feeling, one that has been uttered by Jesus himself, whose unique closeness to God as his Abba/Father makes his desperate question of why God has abandoned him all the more poignant and incomprehensible.

Jesus' second cry expresses his total trust in God in the depths of God's abandonment of him. Into God's loving hands Jesus entrusts his life, in spite of, or perhaps because of his utter despair. It is very interesting that in his second cry Jesus addresses not "God" but "Father." Perhaps it is Jesus' total despair that enables him to see "God" differently: not as a remote and unfeeling all-powerful deity, but as a near, loving, and all-compassionate Father whose hands will catch him as he falls into the abyss of death. As we lie dying, we are encouraged by Jesus' second try to put our trust and our lives into the hands of our Father/Mother. We are invited to let ourselves fall into the womb of the Father's mercy (*rahamim*), the abyss of his love (*hesed*) and the trustworthiness of his promise (*emet*), not because we have convincing proofs of God's existence and the immortality of our souls, or because of the good things we have done, but only because of the solidity and trustworthiness of God's promise and on the basis of what God has done in and for his Son Jesus and throughout human history. This confidence in God is not the fruit of an intellectual understanding but a final expression of our faith and hope and love. I suggested above that Jesus' total darkness and despair on the cross enables him to see God as his Father. I think something similar will happen to us. As we mourn the loss of our loved ones, the sadness and emptiness we feel open up a clearing in the dark forest of our lives where God's light may shine and bring warmth to our grieving hearts, because God is the Father who has mourned the unjust death of his beloved Son. And when our turn comes, as we lie dying in pains and fear, the inescapable loneliness and darkness surrounding death and dying beckon us to remember that we are not alone in this last stage of our journey: the Son of God has gone this way before us and is now walking by our side.

Jesus' third cry expresses the fulfillment of his life: it is "finished." In spite of the apparent failure of his mission and the ignominious end of life, Jesus' life is not wasted or meaningless. God has given Jesus a task to perform, that is, bringing about the reign of God, and he did complete it. The final cry "It is finished" is both a triumphant and joyful acknowledgment of the successful completion of a difficult mission. It is the equivalent of "I did it!" or "Mission accomplished!" It is important to note the difference between "finish" and "end." "End" is merely a chronological termination; "finish" signifies completion and consummation. Our death too is not as just the end but the fulfillment of a life project. The 'end' is simply the termination of a story, as we are told at the end of a film. It is merely a period after a sentence. When we utter at the end of our lives, as Jesus did: "It is finished," we mean something much more than the chronological stop. Rather we cry out in triumph and joy: "I did it!" We mean that our lives are not just random stories; rather they are parts of a history, indeed a cosmic history, with an ultimate meaning, which for now we do not see, but we trust that there is. "Finished" does not mean "ended," much less "stopped," to be resumed somewhere else, but "fulfilled" and "consummated." Despite the apparent failures of our lives, dreams not lived, roads not taken, projects not completed, we can utter at the end of our lives, in joy and thanksgiving: "It is completed, by the grace of God." Thus, in his ministry and his death for the sake of the kingdom of God, Jesus shows us not only how to live but also how to die. He gives us both the *ars bene moriendi* (the art of dying well) and the *ars bene vivendi* (the art of living well).

5

FROM DEATH TO RESURRECTION

WHAT HAPPENS IN THE MEANTIME?

One question that keeps nagging those who hold both the immortality of the soul and the resurrection of the dead at the end of time concerns the condition of those who have died. Except Jesus who died and was raised to life only three days after his death, and Mary who is believed to have been assumed into heaven immediately after she ended her earthly existence, those who have died face a period of extremely long time between their deaths and the time of bodily resurrection. Suppose the first *homo erectus* died some 1.8 million years ago, where and how has her soul existed since then until her body is raised from the dead, perhaps billions of years from now? This in-between period is called the 'intermediate state,' and the mode of existence of the soul is the 'separated soul' (*anima separata*).

At first sight, the existence of the intermediate state and of the separated soul seems to be a teaching of the Catholic Church. In a passage already cited in the last chapter, *Catechism of the Catholic*

Church: "The Church teaches that every spiritual soul is created immediately by God—it is not 'produced' by the parents—and also that it is immortal: it does not perish when it separates from the body at death, and it will be reunited with the body at the final Resurrection." (§366). Four points are being made here: first, the immediate creation of the human soul by God; second, its immortality; third, the separation of the soul from the body at death; and fourth, the soul's reunion with the body at the universal resurrection.

The above text seems to espouse a dualism between body and soul: the body is said to be "produced" by the parents, whereas the soul is "created immediately by God," implying thus two distinct origins and agents; the body is corruptible whereas the soul is immortal; at death the soul is separated from the body; and in the intermediate state the soul maintains a separate existence until it is "reunited with the body at the final Resurrection." Indeed, Christian anthropology has often been accused, especially by feminists, of being infected by Platonic dualism, with its loathing for matter, the body (especially female), and sexuality. That there has been in the Christian tradition a longstanding abhorrence for these realities and that this dualistic/Manichaean view was bolstered by Greek philosophy is beyond question. A cursory reading of Origen, one of the great Greek theologians, or Augustine, one of the great Latin ones, will dispel any lingering doubt in this matter.

Before examining further this dualism in Catholic anthropology, it is to be noted that *Catechism*, despite its apparent dualistic language, unequivocally affirms the ontological unity of the human person: "The unity of soul and body is so profound that one has to consider the soul to be the 'form' of the body: i.e., it is because of its spiritual soul that the body made of matter becomes a living, human body; spirit and matter, in man, are not two natures united, but rather their union forms a single nature" (§365). The last sentence of this statement is extremely important: According to *Catechism*, "matter" and "spirit" in humans are not two already complete, independently existing "natures" that subsequently join together to form another "nature," that is, the human nature, but rather there is only *one* "nature" (the human nature) which comes into being out of the union of the two *constituents* (not two already existing "natures").

In support of this position, *Catechism* cites a text from the Second Vatican Council's Pastoral Constitution on the Church in the Modern World (*Gaudium et Spes*): "Man, though made of body and soul, is a unity. Through his very bodily condition he sums up in himself the elements of the material world.... For this reason man may not despise his bodily life. Rather he is obliged to regard his body as good and to hold it in honor since God has created it and will raise it up on the last day" (§364). To understand the theological basis of the Catholic Church's positive attitude toward the human body as expressed by Vatican II, which serves as a corrective to the church's past dualistic anthropology, a brief overview of the teaching of the Bible is helpful.

Since the concept of *anima separata* presupposes a view of the human being as composed of body and soul, I first examine what the Bible and Christian Tradition say about the nature of the human person. I next discuss whether we must accept the existence of the intermediate state and the separated soul. I end with reflections on the belief in the reincarnation.

Biblical and Christian View of the Human Person

The Biblical Teaching on the Human Person

Ironically, the concept of 'spiritual soul,' which is central in Christian anthropology, does not have an equivalent in the Bible. The Hebrew term *nephesh*, commonly translated as 'soul,' comes closest to it. However, it does not mean 'soul' in the Christian sense as explained above, but the throat as the seat of vital needs, desire and feelings, life itself, or a living being. The Greek version of the Hebrew Bible (the Septuagint) translates it with *psychē*, which in turn is (mis)-rendered into English as *soul*. In the New Testament, *psychē* refers to the physical life of an animal or a human being, the life principle, the human person as a whole (in the modern sense of "self"), or the moral self. At times it can mean something distinct from the body (*sōma*), as in Jesus' warning: "Do not fear those who kill the body but cannot kill the soul; rather fear him who can destroy both soul and body in hell" (Mt 10:28). In this case, *psychē* means something other than the physical life, since it cannot be killed by human beings.

Paul uses at least six different terms to describe the human being as a whole, each referring to the *entire person* but under various but not mutually opposing and exclusive aspects:

(1) *Sōma* (body) is the person as a whole, a living and unified organism, the modern "self," but with emphasis on the material component.

(2) *Sarx* (flesh, equivalent to the Hebrew *basar*) is the human person as a natural, physical, earth-bound being, prone to being opposed to God and the things of God.

(3) *Psychē* (soul) indicates the human being as a living being with conscious, purposeful activities. It is not yet the life with and in God or the Spirit of God. Like *sarx*, *psychē* is the human person seen as opposed to the life in the Spirit of God: the *psychikos* person or the flesh is contrasted with the *pneumatikos* person or the person animated by the Holy Spirit (1 Cor 15:44-49).

(4) *Pneuma* (spirit) is the human person who in his knowledge and freedom is open to receiving the Holy Spirit. In 1 Thess 5:23, in his prayer for the Thessalonian Christians, Paul enumerates three elements together, suggesting that they make up the human being: "May your spirit (*pneuma*) and soul (*psychē*) and body (*sōma*) be kept sound and blameless at the coming of our Lord Jesus Christ."

(5) *Kardia* (heart) is the human person as the seat of knowledge and emotions.

(6) *Nous* (mind) is the human being as a knowing and judging

subject, capable of intelligence, planning and decision. Clearly, the Catholic concept of soul comprises all these six elements of Pauline anthropology.

In addition to *nephesh*, the Hebrew Bible uses the word *ruah* to refer to the human person. Literally meaning 'breath' and 'wind,' *ruah* refers to the human person as a living being. (The Latin word for *ruah* is *anima*, which also literally means 'breath' and 'wind' and is figuratively used to mean 'soul.') The life principle in humans is seen not as something they possess by nature but as a gift of God. It is derived from the breath of God, as is stated in Gen 2:7: "The Lord God formed man from the dust of the ground, and breathed into his nostrils the breath (*ruah*) of life, and the man became a living being."

In the New Testament, *ruah* is rendered with *pneuma* (spirit), and given the intimate connection between God's breath and the human spirit, it comes as no surprise that *ruah* gradually refers to the immaterial part of the human person, that is, the equivalent of 'soul' in the modern sense. Furthermore, when the human spirit is enlivened by the Spirit of God, also called the Holy Spirit, the Spirit of Christ, and the Spirit, the human person acquires a new life which will lead to the resurrection of the body, as Paul puts it: "If the Spirit of him who raised Jesus from the dead dwells in you, he who raised Christ from the dead will give you life to your mortal bodies also through his Spirit that dwells in you" (Rom 8:10-11). Paul calls this resurrected body "the spiritual body" [*sōma pneumatikon*], as opposed to the "natural body" [*sōma psychikon*] (1 Cor 15:44).

Paul does not explicitly speak of the separation of the soul from the body at death. Indeed, the so-called intermediate state was not much of a concern to him since he expected the resurrection of the flesh to occur within his lifetime (1 Cor 15:51). However, he was convinced that at the resurrection, "this perishable body puts on imperishability, and this mortal body puts on immortality" and death will be conquered (1 Cor 15:26; 54-57). Paul does not say what transpires to the soul between a person's death and the resurrection, perhaps because for him the human person is a unitary being, not to be divided into body and soul with the possibility of the soul existing apart from the body.

The most important biblical teaching on the human person is not however about the body and the soul and their ontological unity. Rather it is that humans are created in the *image and likeness of God*, and it is this theme that is central in contemporary Catholic anthropology. The basic text is Gen 1:26-27: "Then God said: 'Let us make humankind in our image (*shelem*), according to our likeness (*demut*) .... So God created humankind in his image, in the image of God he created them; male and female he created them." As the image and likeness of God, humans possess an innate orientation to God. To be human is to tend toward God and become like God as much as possible, just as it is in the nature of a copy to resemble its original as much as possible. Furthermore, as the image and likeness of God, humans, no matter what their conditions are, possess a fundamental and inviolable dignity as persons capable of knowledge and freedom whose basic rights must not be denied but rather promoted. In addition, since humans are created in God's image and likeness in their being male and female, women and men are equal in their dignity and worth, and their sexuality is fundamentally good and holy.

The Body/Soul in the Christian Tradition

This biblical vision of the fundamental unity of the human person was preserved in second-century theologians such as Justin Martyr (100-c.163) and Irenaeus of Lyons (c.130-c.200). For the former, salvation includes not only the preservation of the immortality of the soul but also the gift of immortality to the mortal body. The latter, in his fight against the Gnostics, stresses that the human being is composed of a corruptible body (but called toward immortality) and a soul, that is, the breath of life which enlivens the body, and that both are created in the image and likeness of God. In addition to these two elements there is a third, which however does not belong to the human person by nature but is the gift of God, namely, the

Spirit, who by grace transforms humans into the "perfect human being."

In later centuries, however, this ontological unity of the human person became blurred. Developed within the Hellenistic context, Christian theology was heavily influenced by neo-Platonic philosophy with its dualistic cast and its disdain for matter and sexuality (especially woman). Origen (c. 185-c. 254) taught that from eternity God has created a world of spirits, all equal to each other, endowed with freedom of choice and united with bodies of subtle or ethereal matter. Some of these fell from their spiritual status by neglecting the contemplation of God, and were punished according to the severity of their sins. Those with the lightest culpability became angels, their bodies clothed with the thinnest matter. Those with the greatest culpability became demons, their bodies covered with the heaviest matter. Those in between became humans, their ethereal bodies taking on less heavy bodies like ours. However, by living a Christian life and practicing contemplation, humans can be freed from their heavy bodies and recover their original ethereal condition.

Origen's neo-Platonist anthropology is amended by fourth-and-fifth-century Greek theologians, especially the Cappadocians (Basil of Caesarea, Gregory of Nyssa, and Gregory of Nazianzus). For them it is the entire human being, and not only the soul, that is the image and likeness of God. The bodily condition is not the result of a prehistorical sin but is created as good by God. As such the body has a share in salvation, thanks to the body of Christ, of which Christians are members, especially through the sacraments of baptism and the Eucharist. The Cappadocians do make a distinction between the earthly, *psychikon* stage of the body and its resurrected, eschatological state. The former lies under the power of sin and is corruptible; the latter, which corresponds to God's creative intention, is the goal toward which humans must move.

In the Latin Church, the African theologian Tertullian (c.160-c.225) still maintains the unity of body and soul, and, like Irenaeus, distinguishes between the human soul, which is breath [*afflatus*] of God, and the divine Spirit [*Spiritus*], who is given to Christians. The divine Spirit is not a constitutive part of the human being, but without the Spirit, the human body-and-soul reality is worthless. Nevertheless, Tertullian insists that "the flesh is the hinge of salvation" [*caro salutis cardo*] and that "it is in the flesh, with the flesh, and through the flesh that the soul meditates on everything it meditates in its heart" (*On the Resurrection of the Dead*, XV, 3).

This highly positive appreciation for the flesh and for matter in general is however much weakened by another, vastly more influential, African theologian, Augustine of Hippo (354-430). Augustine posits the existence of an immaterial substance in humans which he calls "spirit." This spirit is to be distinguished from the uncreated Spirit, God, and is created by God in God's image. On the basis of this image Augustine devises an ingenious analogy between the human soul and the Trinity, with memory, intelligence, and love in the soul standing for the Father, the Son, and the Spirit respectively. The superiority of the soul over the body is clearly affirmed; it is only by returning into the soul that one can truly discover God.

Thomas Aquinas (c.1225-1274), following Aristotle's *On the Soul*, especially his teaching on matter and form, corrects the overly dualistic tendency of Augustinian anthropology. For Thomas, the human being is not the union of two independent *substances*, namely, the body and the soul. Rather the body ("matter") and the soul ("form") are the *principles* constituting the *one* substance which is the human person. They are termed "material cause" and "formal cause" respectively; the other two remaining "causes" of each finite being are the "efficient cause" (who makes it) and the "final cause" (the purpose for which it is made). As principles of being, matter and form—in this case, body and soul respectively—cannot exist by themselves but only in union with each other.

In light of Thomas's anthropology, we may say that as "matter" of the soul, the human body "materializes" and individualizes the soul as *this* soul of *this* body, and together they constitute a human being as this person as distinct from that person. As "form" of the body, the soul makes it a *human* body and is its life force or "energy." As "informed" by the soul, the human body is different from all other bodies, that of a dog, for instance, and is to be treated with special reverence, during the funeral rites and even after its dissolution into dust. Together the body and the soul enable the person to carry out their three functions, namely, growing and reproducing (the vegetative power), feeling (the sensitive power), and thinking (the intellective power). Hence, it is in principle impossible for the soul to function apart from the body and to survive the corruption of the body.

However, following the Christian faith, Thomas maintains that after death, the human soul, being spiritual and immortal, exists in a state of separation from the body (*anima separata*) but this existence during this "intermediate state" is unnatural and will end with the resurrection of the dead at the end of time. Thus, the "reunion" of the body and the soul at the resurrection of the dead is something the person naturally longs for, and as long as the two are separated, the person is not yet in full happiness and blessedness, even in heaven now.

Origin of the Soul and the Intermediate State

Whereas the nature of the soul as the form of the body and its immortality are widely accepted in Catholic theology, there remains much debate about its origin and the so-called intermediate state. With regard to the soul's origin, the above-mentioned *Catechism* asserts that "every spiritual soul is created immediately from God" ("creationism"). This position is a corollary of the doctrine that the soul is immaterial; as such it cannot be the result of the material evolutionary process or the reproductive functions of the parents. Whether the soul is created and infused into the embryo at conception, or several weeks later, when it has achieved its vegetative and sensitive functions, as Thomas Aquinas opines, is debated. Those who oppose abortion are generally in favor of immediate animation.

There is however another theory called "traducianism," according to which the soul along with the body is transmitted through the parents. Tertullian and Augustine are the foremost proponents of this theory in antiquity, the latter to strengthen his theology of original sin. Among its opponents are Peter Lombard and Thomas Aquinas, the latter providing an extensive argument for rejecting the view that the soul is "transmitted with the semen, as though it were begotten by coition" (*Summa contra Gentiles* I, chapter 86). It is to be noted however that in itself traducianism does not affirm that the parents "create" the soul of their child but only that they "transmit" it, or are at best its "secondary causes," with God being its "primary cause." The theological advantage of traduciansim over creationism seems to be that the former accounts better for the unity of body and soul.

Concerning the time between death and resurrection, as mentioned above, *Catechism of the Catholic Church* seems to imply that there is an intermediate state during which the soul exists separated from the body until it is reunited with the body at the final resurrection. Immediately after death the souls of those who die in God's grace and are perfectly purified go to heaven, "the ultimate end and fulfillment of the deepest human longings, the state of supreme, definitive happiness" (§1024). On the contrary, "immediately after death the souls of those who die in a state of mortal sin descend into hell, where they suffer the punishments of hell" (§1035).

Finally, those who die in God's friendship but are still imperfectly purified must go to "purgatory," where they undergo a painful process of purification to be fully worthy of seeing God. This doctrine of purgatory is derived from the church's practice of praying for the dead and commendation of "almsgiving, indulgences, and works of penance undertaken on behalf of the dead" (§1032). Thus, the existence of the intermediate state is thought of as a necessary presupposition for the doctrine on purgatory, which we will discuss in the next chapter.

Reincarnation: A Possibility?

One belief that has become highly popular in the West in recent years is that of reincarnation, perhaps because the Christian doctrine of purgatory is no longer rightly understood, or because there is a fascination with anything taken to be part of Asian religions, or because reincarnation is perceived as a reasonable and even necessary way for the majority of humans to achieve full and complete flourishing. It is in this context that the belief in reincarnation emerges. As I mentioned at the beginning of chapter 3, because not all the consequences of our actions—good and bad—can be reaped as reward or punishment in one single lifetime, however long, we naturally think of the possibility of perhaps one or several more lives after this life in which to complete our task of coming to full salvation.

The concept of reincarnation has an ancient pedigree and is not limited to the so-called "Orient." The Greek philosopher Plato spoke about it; it was present in ancient Egyptian and Roman religions, and even some Christian theologians seem to have entertained it as a possibility. At the heart of reincarnation is the concept of karma, the universal law of cause- and-effect, as inescapable as gravity: good deeds lead to good things, and bad deeds lead to bad things, and bad deeds and bad things must be removed until the human person achieves perfection. In the Hindu and Buddhist belief systems, this process of karma takes the extreme form of the rebirth of the soul in successive life forms until the cycle of death-rebirth-death (*samsara*) is ended by removing the three "unwholesome roots," namely, hatred, craving, and ignorance. Only then is the person liberated (*moksa*) and submerges into Brahman or enters into nirvana.

As to the theory of reincarnation as a way to achieve full perfection, *Catechism of the Catholic Church* states: "Death is the end of man's earthly pilgrimage, of the time of grace and mercy which God offers him so as to work out his earthly life in keeping with the divine plan, and to decide his ultimate destiny.... We shall not return to other earthly lives.... There is no 'reincarnation' after death" (§1013).

A number of theologians have pointed out that there are many similarities between the Hindu and Buddhist teaching on reincarnation and the Christian doctrine on purgatory. Both insist on the necessity of a total spiritual purification of the soul before one is able to enjoy eternal life with God. The difference is that for Christians, this process of purification takes place in this one single life, and if necessary, continues in the life after death, and not in one or more lives on earth again in another body, as in reincarnation.

Yet there is another, much deeper, difference. Whereas Hinduism and Buddhism insist that the process of personal purification must be carried out by each individual by herself or himself, by their own efforts, Christians believe that it can never be accomplished by human efforts alone. These are necessary but not sufficient. The final liberation, the resurrection of the dead and life in the kingdom of God, is ultimately God's own gracious deed, the work of the loving and merciful God.

On the one hand, the Hindu and Buddhist view takes personal responsibility and the moral duty for self-perfection seriously, a doctrine necessary to combat spiritual sloth and particularly salutary in our age when we tend to blame our bad behaviors on others. However, if pushed to the extreme, it may induce self-righteousness (what Christians call "Pelagianism," after the fifth-century British monk who allegedly taught the possibility of salvation by one's own efforts) and despair, because such self-perfection seems forever out of human reach.

The Christian view, on the other hand, fosters faith and hope in God's power and mercy, but it also may lead to spiritual laziness and passivity (which is known as "quietism"). Perhaps rather than accepting either reincarnation or purgatory as mutually incompatible doctrines, we should see them as cautionary tales about human behavior and as a moral imperative to live a good and generous life.

This chapter discusses in detail the questions of body and soul and their ontological unity and the possibility of the intermediate state. For some readers, this philosophical and theological discussion may appear abstract and remote, and indeed the medieval categories of 'matter', 'form,' and 'soul' may sound quaint to modern ears. Yet, it is central for our faith and spirituality, for "living to death" and "dying to life," is to know that our body and our soul are ontologically one, that the one cannot exist fully without the other. We do not have a body or a soul; rather we *are* our body and our soul. Hence, no salvation will bring us perfect happiness unless it involves *both* the body and the soul.

Popular piety often speaks of "salvation of the soul" as if the body does not matter. Yet it is a source of great comfort to know that the body with which we enjoy the delights of food and drink and the ecstasy of lovemaking, the body with which we touch and caress our loved ones and our pets, the body in which we dance and contemplate works of art, the body we rejuvenate with oil and cream, the body we keep healthy though medication and exercise, the body we abuse with alcohol and drugs, the body that wrinkles and sags with age, the body that grows feeble and deformed with illness, and the body that writhes in the agony of impending death, *that body is who we are*, because it is through it that we become eternally who we are, and without it our soul cannot arrive at perfect and eternal joy and peace.

It is perhaps because of this role of the body as the "hinge of salvation" [*caro cardo salutis*], to use Tertullian's celebrated expression, that God has become flesh, taking a very specific body in a particular place and time, born of a Jewish woman, a body that was nourished with Palestinian water and air and foods. It is through this Jewish body, nailed and broken on the cross and present in the eucharistic bread and wine, that Jesus carries out his saving work for all humanity so that we may be incorporated into him, with the hope that our many bodies will be glorified in his one body. That is why in its liturgy the Catholic Church sanctifies the body with holy water, marks with the sign of the cross, venerates with incense, strengthens with oil, and blesses with sacramental celebrations, and why various religions surround the corpses with so many signs of respect and rituals.

6

HEAVEN

A FANTASTICAL SHANGRI-LA?

In the previous chapters we have considered a number of arguments for the possibility of life after death and the need for an analogical or imaginative language to speak about it. We have also reflected on the meaning of our death and dying in the light of Christ's death. In the next two chapters I will deal with the themes that generally people are most curious about when they think of eternal life, namely, heaven and hell.

For clarity's sake I divide the discussion of these themes into two separate chapters. But it is of utmost importance to note that heaven and hell must be viewed together if they are to be rightly understood. My basic thesis is that heaven and hell are not two opposite realities that God creates and then offers to us as two equal options to choose from. Strictly speaking, it is not true that, as the popular saying goes, we can choose either to "go up" to heaven or to "go down" to hell, as if heaven and hell are two parallel destinations for our life journey. Our freedom of choice is not equidistantly poised between heaven and hell as two equally possible and attractive alternatives, as, for example, Italy and France for our vacation. On the contrary, there is only *one* reality for our choice, and that is "heaven."

As infinite goodness and love, God does not and cannot create hell as a kind of Abu Ghraib and then hurl evil people in there after their death to be eternally punished and tortured for their sins. Rather, God offers us *only one* reality, namely, "heaven," that is, the eternal and infinite life and love uniting the three Persons of the Trinity and constituting them the one God. This divine life, or heaven, is what God gives to each and every human being. By contrast, hell is nothing more than the result of a person's irrevocable decision to refuse God's gift of love and cannot be understood except as the contradiction of heaven. Indeed, it is important to note that neither the Apostles' Creed nor the Niceno-Constantinopolitan Creed explicitly mentions hell as an object of belief but only professes faith in "life everlasting" or "the life of the world to come," which are synonymous with heaven. Thus, there is no theological symmetry between statements about heaven and those about hell. We must speak of heaven as *reality* and about hell only as *possibility*, and more precisely, possibility *for me*. The good news that Christianity announces is that in Jesus God has given to all humanity a share in God's being, truth, goodness, and beauty. To put it succinctly, Christians must preach heaven, and not hell.

Heaven as a Fantastic Shangri-la?

Most if not all religions inculcate a firm hope for the state of final and perfect bliss not only for humanity but also the cosmos as a whole, and every religion, as to be expected, presents itself as the best way to achieve it. This state of total fulfillment may be conceived of as immanent to this world (as in Confucianism), or transcending it (as in Hinduism and the three Abrahamic religions, namely, Judaism, Christianity and Islam), as personal union with God (as in theistic religions), or as self-realization (as in non-theistic religions such as

Buddhism), as union-with-and-yet-in-distinction-from the divinity (again, as in the Abrahamic religions) or total identification with the divinity (as in Hinduism). A host of names have been used to refer to this reality of perfect happiness. Chief among these are heaven, paradise, salvation, liberation, beatific vision, total union with God.

Religions dig deep into the human imagination in search of appropriate images and symbols to describe this state of ultimate perfection and total bliss. Saint Paul puts it succinctly, "what no eye has seen, nor ear has heard, nor the human heart conceived, what God has prepared for those who love him" (1 Cor 2:9). Heaven is the reality that both fulfills and exceeds all the desires and hopes of the human heart. When referring to endless possibilities, we often use the popular saying: "The sky's the limit." About heaven, however, the sky is literally no limit to human imagination. The Bible uses a plethora of expressions and images to describe it: God's dwelling, eternal life, glorification, immortality, incorruptibility, light, peace, harmony, banquet, wedding feast, reign with God and Christ, face-to-face vision of God, eternal communion with God and with all humanity, union with Christ in the Spirit, communion with the angels and the saints, our true home, the heavenly sanctuary, the garden of most pleasurable delights (paradise), the heavenly Jerusalem, and so on.

Many religions depict heaven as consisting of several levels or stories. Ancient Judaism and Hinduism speak of seven heavens. Paul relates his experience of being brought up to the third heaven, in his body or out of his body he knows not, into "paradise," where he received "visions and revelations of the Lord" and heard "things that are not to be told, that no mortal is permitted to repeat" (2 Cor 12:1-4). These descriptions of a multi-storied heaven are of course not to be taken as geographical maps or architectural layouts of the place where God and the saints dwell. Rather they hint at the distance separating God and humans and the need for gradual spiritual purification to come near and dwell with the all-holy and all-perfect God.

In hearing these descriptions of heaven, skeptics and atheists will object that they are no more than childish fantasies of wish-fulfillment. Heaven is a sort of Shangri-la, an impossible place where all human desires are realized and perfect happiness achieved. It deserves to be called an "utopia," in both senses of the word, that is, a "good place" and a "no place." Like God, who dwells there, heaven, skeptics and atheists would say, is nothing but a fantastic projection of the human mind and heart. Recognized as such, heaven would be a harmless mental game or mythology, but it can be extremely dangerous, in Karl Marx's famous phrase, "the opium of the masses," when it is manipulated by the powerful to divert the attention of the oppressed people from their enslavement and their struggle for freedom and to console them with a hope of perfect but illusory happiness in heaven.

In response to this critique, it must be honestly acknowledged that the Christian belief in heaven has sometimes been misused as a balm to soothe the pains and sufferings of the marginalized and to stifle their desire for social justice with the promise of a better future in the world to come.

It is no less true however that the hope for heaven has an immense power for social and political transformation when it is properly understood, not as a reward in the afterlife for accepting with patience and resignation the evils in this world presumed to be the will of God, but as the reality, albeit partial, of a transformed existence in justice and peace. This reality, already initiated here and now in this world, impels people of all faiths to live in faith, hope and love in and for God and to work for a better society in effective solidarity with one another.

History is replete with examples of Christians as well as believers of other faiths (and unbelievers as well) who live their lives in pursuit of justice and peace for all, and who derive from their hope for heaven, which is called by various names in different religious traditions, an impetus and a sustenance for their struggle for equality and peace, especially when the outcome is not quickly forthcoming and the temptation to give up is well-nigh irresistible.

It is inevitable therefore that when speaking of heaven Christians make use of images and symbols—the stuff our imagination is made of—that are not different from those used by utopian thinkers, novelists, and poets. This imaginative language, which sometimes borders on science fiction, is found in the Bible itself, especially in the apocalyptic writings, and is widely used in subsequent Christian theology, literature, and art. Colleen McDannell and Bernhard Lang, in their book *Heaven: A History*, suggest that the Christian language about heaven embodies two basic ideas: heaven as an intimate union with and contemplation of God (the "theocentric" concept of heaven), and heaven as a reunion with and enjoyment of the company of one's loved ones such as spouses, children, relatives and friends (the "anthropocentric" concept of heaven). In what follows I will develop these two motifs of heaven.

Heaven as Face-to-Face Vision of God

The first thing *Catechism of the Catholic Church* says about heaven is that it is a face-to-face vision of God: "Those who die in God's grace and friendship and are perfectly purified live for ever with Christ. They are like God for ever, for they 'see him as he is,' face to face" (§1023). *Catechism* refers to three New Testament texts (1 Jn 3:2; 1 Cor 13:12; Rev 22:4). All of these texts describe our current knowledge of God as dim, like in a mirror, not direct but mediated through material things, and partial; by contrast they describe our knowledge of God in heaven as clear, direct, immediate, face-to-face, and full, because then we will know God "even as [we] have been fully known" (1 Cor 13:12). In heaven we will see God "as he is" (1 Jn 3:2) for "the Lord will be [our] light," (Rev 22:4), by which we see God.

It is interesting to note how in the Bible there is a gradual progression from *hearing* God's word in prophetic revelation to *seeing* God's face, first in the flesh of Jesus, and finally in heaven. Theologians refer to this seeing of God face-to-face as *beatific vision*, literally a seeing that makes one happy. Pope Benedict XII declared in

1336 that "since the passion and death of the Lord Jesus Christ, the souls [of the blessed] have seen and see the divine essence with an intuitive vision and even face to face, without the mediation of any creature by way of object of vision; rather the divine essence immediately manifests itself to them, plainly, clearly, and openly [*nude, clare et aperte*], and in this vision they enjoy the divine essence." Pope Benedict's language, with expressions such as "the divine essence," "intuitive vision," "without the mediation of any creature," "object of vision," and "plainly, clearly, and openly" may sound very abstract and cold to us today. Indeed, it reflects the mode of speaking of the scholastic theology of the late Middle Ages. But the pope's point is well-taken: In heaven we enter into a most intimate, loving, direct, personal communion with God in God's threefold reality of Father, Son, and Spirit. We experience God the Father/Mother as our Father/Mother; we experience God the Son as our Brother/Sister; and we experience God the Spirit as our Power/Energy, without anything standing in-between as a veil or a curtain hiding God from us. We can of course speak of this personal experience and relationship between us as persons on the one hand and God as Persons on the other as an act of direct knowing, or "seeing," analogous to our direct knowing and seeing persons and things in this world.

In daily life we tend to prize seeing someone over hearing her or him. Of all the five senses, sight seems to give us the most accurate and complete knowledge of persons and things. In the popular Indian story of the six blind men and the elephant, it seems that the true reality of the elephant as a whole can be known only by the narrator who enjoys sight. No wonder then that when we are separated from our loved ones, we would like to communicate with them, at least by phone (and now by texting), but if possible, we prefer to see them through Skype or FaceTime as we talk. Of course, the ideal thing is to see our loved ones in person, face to face, without any intermediary, technological or otherwise.

Because God is spirit, we cannot "see" God with our physical eyes. That is why, when we speak of seeing God face-to-face, we refer to it as "knowledge." But this knowledge of God in heaven is different from the knowledge of God we have here and now. As finite beings that live in the world, we know everything, including God, through the mediation of things. Our current knowledge of God, even though true, remains blurred, since we now know God not as God is in Godself, but as reflected in God's creation. This is what Saint Paul means when he says that we now know God as "in a mirror." In heaven, however, we know God as in himself, not through any mediating thing or image, but directly and immediately. Since the human mind is finite and incapable of this immediate and direct seeing or knowing God, its capacity needs to be enhanced by God's gift of God's own knowledge of himself. This divine knowledge of Godself, by means of which we know God in heaven, is called the "light of glory."

Heaven as Union with the Trinity

As mentioned above, the point of the description of heaven as beatific vision or intuitive knowledge of God is to highlight its nature as a personal union with God, and more precisely, with God as a trinity of persons. Here I would like to develop this concept of heaven a bit further. When humans are enabled by God to participate in the divine life, which Christians call "grace," they do not do so in a generic way, so that one may say, for instance, that they are children of God, without any difference as to whether it is God the Father, God the Son, or God the Spirit we are referring to. On the contrary, it must be said that in grace humans do not have a generic relationship to the divine essence but a proper and truly differentiated relationship to each of the three divine persons. By virtue of this relationship, the human individual is the son or daughter of the Father (and not of the Son or the Spirit), the brother or sister of the Son (and not of the Father or the Spirit), and the temple of the Holy Spirit (and not of the Father or the Son). Thus, these relationships are not interchangeable. Consequently, we cannot pray to God as to the divine essence in a generic sense; rather, we pray to

God the Father, the Son, and the Spirit in different ways. As Saint Paul puts it elegantly, "for through him [the Son] we both [Jews and gentiles] have access in one Spirit to the Father" (Eph 2:18).

In light of this personal and differentiated relation of human beings to each of the three divine Persons, heaven is not to be understood as an indiscriminate and undifferentiated intuitive vision of the one "divine essence," as Pope Benedict XII puts it, and as is commonly thought, but rather as a perfectly fulfilled and distinct relationship of knowledge and love with the Father in the Son and by the power of the Spirit. In other words, in heaven we are given an eternal and irrevocable share in the life of the Trinity itself. Thus, in heaven we relate to God the Father with the same filial love with which the Son is related eternally to his Father, and we do so by the same power as that with which the Father and the Son relate to each other in mutual knowledge and love (that is, the Spirit).

This is the most mind-blowing truth about the afterlife according to the Christian faith: In heaven we live a life no less divine than God the Father, God the Son, and God the Spirit do. To use the language favored by Orthodox theology, grace, the fulfillment of which is heaven, is the divinization or deification (*theōsis*) of humans because by grace we live, albeit in a finite manner, the very life of the Trinity. What the triune God is by nature, we are by grace.

Heaven as Communion with the Whole Humanity

The second aspect of heaven which, as we have mentioned above, Colleen McDannell and Bernhard Lang call the "anthropocentric" concept of heaven, concerns our relationship with our fellow human beings. I suggest heaven may be imagined as a reunion with one's loved ones. In fact, in the Christian understanding, the loved ones include not only those people who are close and known to us, such as spouses, family members, and friends, but all the angels and the saints, and indeed all humans who have been saved (the blessed). Among the saints, Mary of course stands out in preeminence, given her special role in the history of salvation. Mary's husband Joseph too would be among the first to greet and welcome us.

In addition to those who have been canonized by the church, there are those—from the first human being to the last—who have died in communion with God, most of whom are unknown to us. Human imagination is staggered beyond all telling when it tries to come up with their number. The author of Revelation refers to their praise of God as "the voice of a great multitude, like the sound of many waters and like the sound of mighty thunder peals" (19:6). This "great multitude" is made up of billions and billions upon billions of human beings, from the first day of the emergence of humanity into history ("Adam" and "Eve") to the day when the last human dies and history ends. Strangers though they were to us whose existence we could not even surmise in our wildest dream, we now come to know and love them as members of the one family of God, as our brothers and sisters, with whom we enter into a boundless and eternal communion.

Among the "great multitude" in heaven, I make bold to suggest, we will find, to our utter surprise but also immense joy, non-Catholic Christians, non-Christian believers such as Jews, Muslims, Hindus, Buddhists, Jains, Sikhs, and the followers of other religious traditions, and even non-believers, whom in our smallness of mind and narrowness of heart we think God's infinite love and mercy cannot embrace, but whose goodness and holiness not rarely far exceed ours and is known to God alone. This all-inclusive vision of heaven is no fevered concoction of wishy-washy, kumbaya-singing bleeding liberal hearts. It has been proposed by no higher church authority than the Second Vatican Ecumenical Council itself in paragraph 16 of the Dogmatic Constitution on the Church (*Lumen Gentium*).

Heaven can thus be pictured as an endless and joyous reunion of the entire human family, in which hostility and hatred cease, unconditional forgiveness is given, universal reconciliation brought about, and complete happiness achieved. We are infinitely happy not simply because of our own eternal blessedness but also because of the eternal happiness of others, even of those we once condemned as wicked and sinful and eternally lost. Where and when this final blessedness of all humanity will occur, we will consider in chapter 9, where we consider the end of the world, and in the last chapter, when we imagine "a new heaven and a new earth." For now, suffice to note that the two aspects of heaven, "theocentric" and "anthropocentric," are not opposed to each other. Indeed, they stand in direct proportion with each other, that is, the more united we are with the Triune God, the more united we are with the whole humanity, and vice versa. To these two dimensions of heaven I will add a third, the "cosmocentric," as the universe itself, in all its material reality, will be transformed in this heaven, as we will see in the last chapter.

Perhaps there is no better way to end our reflections on heaven than glancing at one of the greatest epics of world literature, the Italian Dante Alighieri's *Divina Commedia*. Written between 1308 and its author's death in 1321, it is composed of three canticas titled *Inferno*, *Purgatorio*, and *Paradiso* respectively. It is an allegory of the soul's ascent to God, from hell through purgatory to paradise. Dante is guided by the Roman poet Virgil from hell through purgatory, and is then guided by Beatrice through the nine concentric and spherical circles of heaven. The first seven heavenly spheres deal with the four cardinal virtues—prudence, fortitude, justice, and temperance—and are represented by the Moon, Mercury, Venus, the Sun, Mars, Jupiter, and Saturn. The eighth sphere, represented by the fixed stars, is inhabited by those who possess the three theological virtues of faith, hope and love. The ninth sphere, or the Primum Mobile, is inhabited by the angels. Topping the nine spheres is the Empyrean, which is the dwelling-place of God. Upon arriving in paradise, Dante meets and converses with great saints such as Thomas Aquinas, Bonaventure, Peter, and John. In the thirty-third and final canto of *Paradiso*, Dante comes face to face with the Triune God—Father, Son, and Spirit—appearing as three equally large circles, each with a different color, occupying the same space. Within these three circles Dante discerns the human form of Christ. Dante tries to understand how the three circles fit together and how the humanity of Christ relates to the divinity of the Son, but confesses his total inability to do so ("that was not a flight for my wings"). However, in a flash of understanding, Dante realizes that God's love is the force that moves all things:

> *But already my desire and my will*
> *were being turned like a wheel, all at one speed,*
> *by the Love which moves the sun and the stars.*

Heaven is where God's love, "which moves the sun and the stars," saves and transforms all things and brings them into God's eternal and Trinitarian life.

7

ETERNAL HELL

A CONTRADICTION TO GOD'S LOVE?

If there is an eschatological theme that is almost impossible to talk about, it is certainly hell. Part of the reason for this is that, as I mentioned in the last chapter, hell is not a positive reality that God creates as an alternative to heaven for us to choose from, but an absence of reality, and of course it is well-nigh impossible to speak meaningfully about something that is not. In a true sense, everything that can be said about hell has already been said, albeit inversely, in what we have said about heaven. If, as we have seen in the last chapter, heaven is immediate vision of God, personal communion with the Trinity, and union with all humanity, then hell is total ignorance of God, permanent separation from the triune God, and bitter hatred of all. In a nutshell, hell is the absence, or more precisely, the total negation of heaven: Heaven is happiness, hell is misery; heaven is light, hell is darkness; heaven is life, hell is death; heaven is faith fulfilled by vision, hell is ignorance frozen into nescience; heaven is love, hell is hatred; heaven is joy, hell is sadness; heaven is peace, hell is war; heaven is fullness, hell is emptiness; heaven is self-giving openness toward others, hell is selfish curvature into oneself.

Of course, the fact that hell is the negation of heaven does not mean that it is not real or that it cannot be somehow talked about, if only haltingly. It does mean that hell cannot be understood *in and by itself* but only in reference to and by way of contrast with heaven. Indeed, just as only those who have seen the blessing of light can really suffer the curse of darkness; only those have felt joy, peace, fullness, and communion can fathom the depths of sadness, war, emptiness, and isolation, so only those who have lived by faith, hope, and love can truly perceive the pains of ignorance, despair, and hatred; only those who have savored the sweetness of heaven can taste the bitterness of hell. To be sure, the other way works as well: Once we have the misfortune to experience hell, we long all the more earnestly for heaven.

Two Arguments Against Hell

In a certain sense the idea of hell as punishment for evil deeds is neither outrageous nor unfamiliar. Children growing up learn that there are consequences to their actions, and parents instill this idea of cause-and-effect and encourage a sense of moral responsibility by a system of reward and punishment. Civilized societies have a legal system whereby lawbreakers are meted out punishments commensurate to their crimes. The operative word here is of course "commensurate." Furthermore, most people would find commensurate punishments for bad deeds unobjectionable if they are imposed not as a retribution but as a means for moral correction and improvement. It is not for nothing that prison is sometimes called "correctional facility," though sadly what happens there more often than not worsens the moral condition of the inmates.

On both of these aspects of punishment, that is, commensurateness of the penalty and its rehabilitation purpose, the Christian doctrine of hell encounters severe difficulties. First, hell as a punishment consisting in eternal damnation, with never-ending physical, psychological and spiritual pains inflicted upon sinners who have died in the state of mortal sin, does not seem to be a fitting penalty for any evil act that humans can possibly commit. While an evil choice necessarily brings about bad consequences for the person making it, to hold that human freedom, which is by nature finite, limited, and conditioned, can make an irrevocable choice culminating in eternal damnation as its effect would be tantamount to endowing it with an infinite power capable of producing deeds of eternal consequences. Only an infinite being can, it seems, do something infinite, with eternal and never-changing consequences, unless of course this infinite being—God—chooses to turn a finite being's finite guilt into infinite guilt, a limited evil act into an unlimited evil act, which seems to be totally out of God's character.

In response to this objection against the eternity of hell based on the limited nature of human freedom, appeal may be made to the argument advanced by Saint Anselm of Canterbury (1033-1109). In his book on atonement *Cur Deus Homo* (*Why God Became Man*), Anselm argues that the moral quality of an action depends not on the nature of the action itself but rather, in the case of the good deed, on the dignity of the person who does it, and in the case of the bad deed, on the dignity of the person who is sinned against. An identical evil action done by the same person may possess a qualitatively different guilt depending on the rank and dignity of the person against whom it is done, say, a king and a commoner. For example, regicide (killing of a king) bears greater guilt than the murder of a child; it deserves to be—and will be—punished more severely. Thus, according to Anselmian logic, an evil action (sin) committed against the infinite God has an infinite guilt, even though it is done by a finite agent, because of God's infinite greatness and honor.

On the other hand, the goodness of an action comes from neither the nature of the action nor its beneficiary but rather from the dignity of the doer. The same good action done to the same person by two individuals of different rank has a different value. For instance, if I give alms to a poor person and if the king does the same thing to the same person, the goodness of his action is greater than mine because of his greater rank and dignity. Thus, for Anselm, only God's good action can have an infinite goodness, because only God is infinitely great, whereas sins against God, though committed by finite agents, always have an infinite guilt, because the being against whom the sin is committed is an infinite being (God), and therefore deserves an eternal punishment.

Critics argue that Anselm's reasoning only makes sense in the feudal society where social rank and honor determine the moral value of actions. However, in a society where the morality and worth of the action is measured by its nature, and not by the honor of the doer or of the recipient of the action, his argument is not persuasive. Hence, the Christian doctrine of the eternity of hell does not make sense to most if not all people living in democratic societies today.

Secondly, at best one can understand why God may want to inflict pains on sinners as a temporary chastisement, not unlike a limited prison term, to correct them and bring them to conversion. However, to think of hell as a divinely-willed eternal and limitless punishment with no reforming and rehabilitating opportunity for the sinner seems to make God into a vindictive despot. (It is interesting to note that there is a parallel between this argument against the eternity of hell and the current opposition of the magisterium of the Catholic Church to capital punishment, not only because an irreparable mistake might be made in sentencing a wrong person to death, but also because it is purely punitive and vindictive and does not leave any possibility for moral reform.) Against this purely retributive understanding of hell it has been argued that it is incompatible with God's all-merciful and all-forgiving love for all humanity and that it would frustrate God's efficacious will to save all humanity.

These two arguments against hell, especially when it is understood as an eternal punishment, combined with, as we will see, the scarcity of biblical materials on hell, requires us to be extremely circumspect and tentative in speaking about hell, even though of it speak we must. Our theological discourse about hell must therefore eschew the detailed and lurid depictions of it found in arts, such as the Dutch painter Hieronymus Bosch's fantastic portrayal of the various punishments in hell that are custom-designed for each type of sin; in literature, such as Dante's first cantica of his *Divina Commedia*, entitled *Inferno* [Hell], already mentioned in our discussion of heaven; and in the purported mystical visions of hell such as those of Saint John Bosco, Blessed Anne Catherine Emmerich, and Saint Faustina, among a host of others. Such fire-and-brimstone depictions of hell, which are the staple of popular sermons during revival meetings and spiritual retreats, may frighten some sinners to repentance but do little to honor God's merciful justice and forgiving love. My reflections on hell will be guided by what the Bible and Christian Tradition teach about hell and end with some suggestions on how we should think about it today.

The Bible on Hell

The most remarkable thing to be noted with regard to the teaching of the Bible on hell is that how little it says about hell—indeed, all the biblical sayings about hell as eternal punishment after death can be listed on a couple of pages—in contrast to the huge amount of attention it lavishes on heaven. Furthermore, the little the Bible says about hell is far from unambiguous and consistent. Taken literally, as will be mentioned below, the images that are used to describe hell seem to annul one another.

First of all, there is a difficulty with the Hebrew and Greek terms that are translated into English as "hell." There is the Hebrew *sheol*, which in early Hebrew thought means the place beneath the earth where the dead, both the righteous and the unrighteous, dwell, unconscious and silent. It basically means the grave and/or the netherworld. Gradually, however, it takes on the meaning of the realm reserved for the wicked dead and is often depicted as a place deep below the earth, full of gnawing worms, darkness, dust, and silence. Though often translated as "hell," clearly *sheol* does not have the connotations associated with the Christian concept of hell as a place of everlasting torture.

When the Hebrew Bible was translated into Greek, *sheol* was rendered with the word *hadēs* and it too has the connotation of an underground place (the "pit" or the "abyss") of darkness and silence to house the dead. Another Greek term, *gehenna*, which is the transliteration of the Aramaic *gēhinnām*, itself derived from the Hebrew *gē hinnōm* and *gē ben hinnōm*, literally the "valley of (the son) of Hinnon," refers to the valley located on the south slope of Jerusalem where at one time human sacrifices were offered. In the intertestamental period (the 400-year period between the writing of the Hebrew Bible and that of the New Testament), the term came to mean the place where the wicked would receive God's final judgment and eternal punishment. Like *sheol*, it is located in the depths of the earth and is said to include fire, darkness, and the weeping and gnashing of teeth. In the rabbinical literature, *gehenna* is equated to *sheol* and is thought to be the place where the wicked dead receive punishments appropriate to their sins such as idolatry, immorality, arrogance, lack of compassion for the poor, and even excessive listening to women!

The Gospels, which are written in Greek, use both terms *hadēs* and *gehenna*, the former four times (Mt 11:23; 16:18; Lk 10:15; 16:23) and the latter eleven times (Mt 5:22, 29-30; 10:28; 18:9; 23:15, 33; Mk 9:43, 45, 47; Lk 12:5). In addition to these two terms, the Gospels make use of images commonly found in Jewish literature of the period to refer to hell, principally "everlasting fire" and "darkness."

In his preaching, Jesus uses *hadēs* and *gehenna* to refer to the place of punishment for the devil and those who reject God, himself, and the prophets. In addition, those who are guilty of hypocrisy (Mt 23:15, 33), hateful language by calling others "fool" (Mt 5:22), failure to perform one's duties (Mt 24:45-51), sexual immorality (Mt 5:29-30; 18:8-9), and spiritual unfruitfulness (Mt 7:19; 13:40, 42, 50; 25:30) are liable to the punishments of hell, which he describes with the stock-in-trade images of fire, darkness, undying worms, and weeping and gnashing of teeth. Like his contemporaries, Jesus thinks that hell is located in the depths of the earth, as opposed to the heights of heaven. The punishments in hell are said to be "eternal" or "everlasting." For instance, in the famous parable of the final judgment in Matthew 25, Jesus affirms that the wicked will go to "eternal punishment" (*eis kolasin aiōnion*) and the good to "eternal life" (*eis zōen aiōnion*) (Mt 25:46). The everlastingness of hell is also intimated by the "inextinguishableness" of fire and the "undyingness" of the worms.

There are also references to hell in other New Testament books. Curiously, in Acts 1:25, Judas Iscariot is said to have turned aside from his ministry and apostleship "to go to his own place." "His own place" (*ho idios topos*) is commonly assumed to be hell, but this meaning is not certain since the expression in other contexts (for example, Ignatius of Antioch's Letter to the Magnesians 5:1 and Polycarp's Letter to the Philippians 9:2) may mean heaven. At any rate, Acts hardly mentions hell or eternal punishment. Hebrews affirms that a fire will consume the enemies of God (Heb 10:26-27) and that those who hear the word of God but remain "unfruitful ground" (Heb 6:7-8) will be cursed and burned.

The letter of James speaks of the dangers of an evil tongue which will "be set on fire by hell" (*geenna*). In 1 Pet 1:3:19 there is a curious mention that after his death Jesus went to preach to "the spirits in prison," that is, those who did not obey God's admonitions and perished in the universal flood. This statement, in addition to Eph 4:9-10, is perhaps the basis for the belief that Jesus "descended into hell" and preached the gospel even to the dead (1 Pet 4:6) so that they might be saved.

The Book of Revelation affirms that Jesus holds "the key of death and Hades" (1:18) and speaks of the "abyss," a subterranean prison, into which the "dragon, that ancient serpent, who is the devil, or Satan," who has been chained by an angel, is thrown, and his cell is locked for a thousand years (Rev 20:1-3). After the thousand years are over, Satan is released from his prison, and he and his army begin an assault on God's people. But a fire comes down from heaven and devours them. Satan is then thrown into "the lake of burning sulphur," where the false prophet has been thrown, and "they will be tormented day and night for ever and ever" (20:10). Then all the dead will be judged, and after the judgment, "death and Hades will be thrown into the lake of fire" (20:14). Finally, the author of Revelation sees a new heaven and a new earth and the Holy City of Jerusalem coming from heaven. Here the righteous will dwell forever, whereas "for the cowardly, the faithless, the polluted, the murderers, the fornicators, the sorcerers, the idolaters, and all the liars, their place will be in the lake that burns with fire and sulphur, which is the second death (21:8).

After this brief overview of the teachings of the Bible on hell a few readers may be scared by the various scenarios of the punishments in hell. Most, I suspect, will be more confused than terrified. If the biblical sayings on hell are taken at face value, that is, as descriptive reports of what occurs in hell, their various statements do not seem to be mutually consistent. First, with regard to its location: Is hell located in the valley of Hinnon on the south side of Jerusalem, or is it in the deepest part of the earth? If the former, it can't be big enough to house all the wicked dead who we think should go there. If the latter, how should one imagine it if the earth is not square or rectangular but spherical? The center of a spherical earth cannot be the deepest part from any geographical vantage-point. As to the punishments, if there is a blazing fire in hell, how can hell be dark at the same time? And, how can the worms survive that deadly heat? If the dead have no bodies, at least before the resurrection, what do the worms gnaw at? Do the worms get fat after eating those many corpses? Do they reproduce themselves so as to be numerous enough to do the job as the number of the damned increases? As to the gnashing of teeth, will dentures be provided to those who no longer have natural teeth? Where is the lake of fire and burning sulphur to be found? How can its horrible smell be prevented from wafting over to the new heaven and the new earth where the blessed dwell? With regard to the eternity of hell, admittedly the Bible speaks of the "everlasting fire"—although the

Greek term *aiōnios* in some instances simply means "lasting a long period of time" and not "forever and ever." Against the eternity of hell, the two objections mentioned above that arise from the infinite mercy and love of God and the intrinsic finiteness of human freedom cannot be dismissed easily. To them a third may now be added, from the side of the blessed. Can a righteous person be fully and perfectly happy in heaven if one of his or her most loved ones, say, spouse or parent or child, is damned to hell forever, with no chance of salvation?

At this point most if not all readers may think that my imagination is running wild and I am getting silly and absurd. But that is precisely my point: Will those who do not believe in hell not ridicule—and rightly—this Christian doctrine if we keep talking about hell as if the language of the Bible gives a journalistic report of what hell is? On the other hand, what the Bible teaches about hell, as distinct from its imaginative language, cannot and must not be dismissed as outmoded mythology if we want to be faithful to the message of the Bible.

To avoid both dangers, it is important to recall what I said in chapter 1 about the need to read the Bible as a historical document, to recover the world *behind* the text; as a literary work, to discover the world *of* or *in* the text; and as the word of God, to discern the world *in front of* the text. With this triple world in mind, I suggest first of all that all the significant biblical texts about hell, especially those of the New Testament, belong to the kind of writing known in scholarly circles as *apocalyptic literature* (of which Revelation is a prime example; on apocalyptic literature, see chapter 4). The world *behind* the apocalyptic literature is the world of the persecution of God's people and of the end-times when there will be a cosmic struggle between the good and evil forces, between God and God's people on the one hand and Satan and his cohort of demons on the other. Like all other apocalypticists, Jesus believes that the world in which he lives is the eschatological world, the dawning of the reign of God, that he himself ushers in by his ministry, death and resurrection. And like other apocalypticists, to make his audience grasp the seriousness and urgency of his message, Jesus cannot but use the stock-in-trade images of hell that were customary in the apocalyptic literature of his day.

Secondly, in reading the texts on hell, we have to realize that *we ourselves*, and not some other people, are involved in this world *in* and *of* the text; that we ourselves are "the cowardly, the faithless, the polluted, the murderers, the fornicators, the sorcerers, the idolaters, and all the liars" and that unless we repent and change our lives, our "place will be in the lake that burns with fire and sulphur." So, for instance, in the parable of the rich man and Lazarus (Lk 16:19-31), it is said that after his death the beggar Lazarus was carried by the angels to Abraham's side. The rich man was in hell, "where he was in torment." He called out to Abraham to ask him to tell Lazarus to dip the tip of his finger in water and cool his tongue because he (the rich man) was "in agony in this fire." We would miss the entire point of the parable were we to inquire where heaven and hell are located (apparently not too far from each other since the rich man could cry out to Abraham!), what kind of water there is in heaven (Evian?), and what kind of fire it is that tormented the rich man (wood-burning?). Jesus is not interested in giving us a description of heaven and hell and the otherworldly water and fire; rather he wants to affirm that God loves in a special manner the poor and the downtrodden whom our society despises and neglects, and that we must listen to his witness to and message about the reign of God and not rely on the miracle of someone coming back to life after death. Furthermore, we must see ourselves as the rich man and not as poor Lazarus, and think seriously about the strong probability that we may end up like him, in "hell."

Thirdly, the biblical texts on hell as the Word of God open up a new world for us, the world *in front of* the text, which we are beckoned to enter. We are called to respond *here and now*, and not at some moment after death, to Jesus' message about the reign of God. This world of justice, peace, love, and compassion, especially for the least and the last and the lost among us, and the integrity of creation, is one that all of us, even those who do not believe in hell, are called to work for. We accept to make this world *in front of* the text a reality for all humanity, not because we fear that we will otherwise be tortured by everlasting fire, pitch-black darkness, weeping and gnashing of teeth, the gnawing by undying worms, and the lake of burning sulphur, but because that is the way we can respond to God's love for us that is manifested in Jesus.

Will All Be Saved?

With these considerations in mind it is gratifying to note that *Catechism of the Catholic Church* is quite restrained in its statement on hell: "The teaching of the Church affirms the existence of hell and its eternity. Immediately after death the souls of those who die in a state of mortal sin descend into hell, where they suffer the punishments of hell, 'eternal fire.' The chief punishment of hell is eternal separation from God" (§1035). While the imaginative language of "descend into hell" and "fire" are still used, *Catechism* does not specify the location of hell nor the nature of its fire. More importantly, it helpfully and succinctly explains the nature of the punishment in hell as "separation from God."

Hell as "separation from God" is the negation of heaven which is, as we have seen in the last chapter, communion with the Trinity and with the whole of humanity. Hell consists in being cut off from communion with others, a pain readily understood today in our world of constant and immediate connection in which it is impossible to imagine ourselves as severed from our network of relationships, however thin and fragile. Given this view of hell as being cut off from all relationships ("excommunicated"), ice, rather than fire, is, I submit, a more telling image of hell. "Hot" can be a compliment, meaning highly desirable, attractive, and even sexy, but "icy" suggests physical distance and emotional coldness that not even the warmth of love can thaw.

There is however one aspect of hell that calls for a closer examination, namely, its eternity. As mentioned above, hell understood as the painful consequence of one's bad action does not constitute a problem; rather the scandal of hell is its eternity. While it is to be acknowledged that in Christian Tradition the eternity of hell has been repeatedly affirmed, especially following Saint Augustine and Saint Thomas, there are also in the early church two other views that argue that hell is not eternal. The first, expounded by the second-century Saint Irenaeus, affirms that God alone is eternal and that eternal life or immortality is a gift of God, and not a natural attribute of any creature, including humans. The implication of this view, known as "conditioned immortality," is that if no creature is naturally eternal, so too is hell. It follows then that by nature hell cannot last forever but will only last as long as evil lasts, and since evil will ultimately be conquered by God, hell will also be destroyed.

The second is known as "universalism," or "universal restoration," derived from the Greek *apocatastasis*, meaning "restoration," "recovery." This term occurs only once in the New Testament, in Peter's speech after the healing of a crippled beggar. Peter urged his fellow Jews to repent and turn to God to have their sins forgiven, so that God may send them the Messiah, namely Jesus, "who must remain in heaven until the time of universal restoration" (Acts 3:21). Peter does not explain what he means by "universal restoration" (*apocatastasis pantōn*). From other New Testament texts such as Col 1:20, 1 Cor 13:21-28, and Rom 5:18; 11:32, its meaning seems to be that God's will to save all will at the end of time reach and save all, even the last of sinners, and that all things will be reconciled with God. Then, as Paul says, "all things are subjected to him [Jesus], then the Son himself will also be subjected to the one who puts all things in subjection under him, so that God may be all in all" (1 Cor 15:28).

The above-cited New Testament texts are often appealed to by later Fathers of the Church, especially Origen, Gregory of Nazianzus, and Gregory of Nyssa, to support the view that there will be universal salvation. This universalism is also taught by many later theologians, especially those who belong to the Anabaptist and

Pietist traditions and the members of the Unitarian Universalist Churches.

Universalism was condemned at the Council of Constantinople in 553, if it is asserted as an indisputable *fact*, as allegedly taught by Origen. But it is not condemned if it is presented as an object of *hope* and *prayer*. In connection with hell there are two truths that must be held together. On the one hand, there is the truth of God's judgment of my actions and the real possibility of damnation for *me*. On the other hand, there is the truth of God's merciful love and will to save all. These two truths cannot be brought into a harmonious and consistent synthesis. But it is important to remember, as I have pointed out in the last chapter, that heaven and hell are not two parallel and equal options God creates for us to choose. God only creates or better, *is* heaven. That's the only option for us to choose or reject. But even in the abyss of our rejection of God, God's saving mercy and love remains all-powerful and victorious. The Pietist theologian C. G. Barth (1799-1862), not the celebrated Swiss Karl Barth (1886-1968), has famously said: "The person who does not believe [universal salvation] is an ox, but the person who teaches it is an ass." Ox and ass we certainly do not want to be, in matters theological as well as in other areas of life.

Among Catholic theologians, Karl Rahner and Hans Urs von Balthasar have suggested that Christians must hope and pray that no one will be damned forever. We cannot *assert* as a dogmatic truth that no one shall be damned forever, but we certainly may, and must, *hope* and *pray* that this will be the case. The basis for this hope is not bleeding-heart liberalism or naive optimism, much less a denial of human freedom and the radicality of evil. Rather it is rooted in what God has promised and has done in Jesus. No one has expressed this conviction more eloquently than Paul: "Death has been swallowed up in victory. Where, O death, is your victory? Where, O death, is your sting?" (1 Cor 15:54-55). Paul never speaks of "hell" but regularly of "death" (Greek, *thanatos*). For him, "the wages of sin is death" (Rom 6:23), not hell. Thus, for him, death is the equivalent of hell. By denying the ultimate victory to death, Paul thereby denies it to hell. For Paul, God's ultimate purpose is that "God may be all in all" (1 Cor 15:28), that "all things will be united in Christ" (Eph 1:10), and that "all things will be reconciled to him, whether on earth or in heaven" (Col 1:20).

The French philosopher Jean-Paul Sartre famously says that hell is the other, by which he means that in the mere presence of others we are forced to see ourselves as an object and to see ourselves as we appear in the world of others. The best way to understand hell, I suggest, is to begin to see ourselves and others not as subject-object in mutual opposition but as a community of friendship and love. Hell begins when the other is perceived as a threat to our well-being, and so we are tempted to create a hell for them. On the contrary, I must begin with the deep realization that *I am hell* if I think there must be a hell for others simply because they are different from me. The possibility of hell lies with me first. Then I pray and hope and act so that there will be no hell, first for others, *then also for me.*

The fourteenth-century English mystic Julian of Norwich (c.1343-c.1416) affirms that behind the reality of hell lies a greater mystery of God's love. She believes that sin serves to lead us to self-knowledge and to accept our need for God. For Julian, God has no wrath but only compassion. Jesus may be spoken of as "Mother" and thus expresses the motherly face of God. Because of all this, she says, God has revealed to her: "All shall be well, and all shall be well, and all manners of things shall be well." This is the hope that should be the source of inspiration for our life and the conviction upon which we must act. Hell is a real possibility because we choose to make it so, but a possibility I can and must annihilate first for others, then for myself, so that "all manners of things shall be well."

8

RESURRECTION OF THE DEAD

RESUSCITATION OR TRANSFORMED LIFE?

No one has better expressed the centrality of the resurrection of Jesus and our own resurrection in the Christian faith and the intrinsic connection between these two realities than Paul: "Now if Christ is raised from the dead, how can some of you say there is no resurrection of the dead? If there is no resurrection of the dead, then Christ has not been raised, and if Christ has not been raised, then our proclamation has been in vain and your faith has been in vain.... If Christ has not been raised, your faith is futile and you are still in your sins" (1 Cor 15:12-17).

The focus of this chapter is the resurrection of the dead in general, and not the resurrection of Jesus, but as Paul makes it clear, we cannot speak of the former without referring to the latter since it is the latter that makes the former possible. Note that Paul's argument is not that Jesus' resurrection is made possible by the resurrection of the dead. Rather it is the opposite: The resurrection of the dead is a reality because there *has been* one instance of it, namely, the resurrection of Jesus. Furthermore, it is the resurrection of Jesus that is the beginning of and the guarantee for the resurrection of the dead. As Paul puts it, "Christ has been raised from the dead, the first fruits of those who have died" (1 Cor 15:20). The Greek for "first fruits" is *aparchē* and represents a Jewish cultic term in the ritual of offering the first fruits to God (Deut 26:1-11). "First" here means more than first in time, as the first fruits of the season; hence, offering the first fruits to God symbolizes the offering of the entire harvest to God. In this sense, the resurrection of Jesus is not only the first resurrection in time but is the real symbol, that is, the *cause* and the *model* of our own resurrection. Consequently I will first reflect briefly on the resurrection of Jesus and then show how it makes possible the resurrection of all the dead and how what we know about our resurrection does not come from philosophical speculations about the body but is rooted in what the New Testament says about the resurrected Jesus.

Jesus Is Raised from the Dead

Chronologically, Paul is, according to available evidence, the first to *write*, though certainly not to talk, about the resurrection of Jesus. In his first letter to the Corinthians, usually dated to the early spring of 57, over a decade before the first Gospel was written, Paul says that he has learned about the resurrection of Jesus through the testimony of others, that is, through tradition:

> For I handed on to you as of first importance what I in turn had received: that Christ died for our sins, in accordance with the scriptures, and that he was buried, and that he was raised on the third day in accordance with the scriptures, and that he appeared to Cephas, then to the Twelve. Then he appeared to more than five hundred brothers and sisters at one time, most of whom are still alive, though some have died. Then he appeared to James, then to all the apostles. (1 Cor 15:3-7).

Paul's statement is the most concise summary of the earliest message of the apostolic preaching about Jesus, which he considers as "of first importance": his death, burial, resurrection, and apparitions to various people. We know however that the accounts given in the four Gospels of what happened to Jesus after his death contain a lot more details than Paul's bare listing of the four facts. Among the most important details omitted is the empty tomb, about which we will speak more shortly. Furthermore, the four accounts present some conflicting reports, especially with regard to the people to whom Jesus appeared after his resurrection. It is interesting to note that the early Christian preaching, at least as transmitted to Paul, omits the fact that Jesus appeared first to Mary Magdalene and other women, even before he appeared to Peter and the other apostles, most probably because women's witness was judged not of legal value. (One wonders whether Mary would not have been terribly upset if Jesus had not appeared to his mother first!)

These discrepancies notwithstanding, all the New Testament writers are in complete agreement on the fact that Jesus has been raised from the dead and that the resurrection is something that happened to Jesus personally, and not something that happened to his disciples as an act of auto-suggestion or mass hallucination. In fact, the disciples are repeatedly described as unwilling to believe in Jesus' resurrection (Mt 28:17; Lk 24:11, 37; Mk 16:11, 14; Jn 20:25). To say that the resurrection of Jesus is real is however not to say that it is amenable to empirical verification, for instance, by means of a camera or a video recorder, in the way his death on the cross was. Indeed, while the Gospels do provide the details of the crucifixion of Jesus, they do not offer any description of the event of Jesus' resurrection itself but only tell of its impact on his disciples. Interestingly, Jesus did not appear to those who had him killed to boast that he was alive; indeed, it is only in faith that his disciples could recognize that he was raised from the dead.

Even the empty tomb, by itself, is not an incontrovertible proof of Jesus' resurrection. As we have seen above, the earliest Christian message as reported by Paul does not explicitly mention the empty tomb, though it might be said to be implied between the phrase "he was buried" and the phrase "he was raised." The absence of the mention of the empty tomb in the earliest kerygma does not necessarily mean that the disciples did not know that the tomb was empty, or that the tomb itself was not empty; in fact, all four Gospels assert that it was. It only means either that the empty tomb was not then considered as an irrefutable proof of Jesus' resurrection, or that it was not regarded as an essential part of the kerygma. Interestingly, however, those who were opposed to the affirmation of Jesus' resurrection did not try to disprove the claim that the tomb was empty (something they could have easily done if it were not). Rather, as Matthew reports, the chief priests suggested that the tomb was empty because Jesus' disciples had stolen his body (Mt 28:12-15). In sum, though no proof of Jesus' resurrection, the empty tomb remains a sign and an invitation to believe in Jesus' resurrection.

Clearly, Jesus' resurrection is an event of a unique kind. It is a real event, in the sense that it *happened*, and in this sense, historical. At the same time, there was no eyewitness of it, nor was it described, nor could it be described, like any other everyday happening. In this sense, it is a transcendent, or more accurately, eschatological event ushering in the end-time. It is an event that only faith can bear witness to. Thus, Jesus' resurrection is not a reanimation or resuscitation which could in principle be publicly verified, as in the cases of Jairus's daughter, the young man of Naim, or Lazarus. These three people could be proved to have come back to life in their former bodies, begin another life, and then die again. None of this Jesus did.

With regard to his risen body, Jesus clearly did not take back the same body that he had three days earlier. Strangely, he was not recognized even by those who had been his constant companions who should have been able to do so with great ease. Mary Magdalene mistook him for a gardener, the two disciples on the way to Emmaus thought he was a stranger, and the apostles believed they saw a ghost. It is only after Jesus had uttered certain words or performed certain gestures that his followers recognized him. Clearly, the risen Christ's body was quite different from the one he had before the crucifixion. Jesus is portrayed as being raised by God to glory and in this way having conquered death, the "last enemy." Jesus did not come back to life eventually to die again. Rather he was given a new life in which death, the consequence of sin, is vanquished and in which he was exalted by God and given a name that is above every name so that every tongue will confess that "Jesus Christ is Lord" (Phil 2:11).

Yet he was eventually recognized as the same Jesus, even with the same wounds on his hands and in his side. So in what does Jesus' self-same identity consist, before and after his resurrection, if not in the physical body? This question is important and we will come back to it when we discuss the nature of our own risen bodies and our own self-identities before death and after the resurrection. For now suffice it to note that the risen Christ's body, though transformed, appears to his disciples as being real and physical: they could see, touch, hear and speak to, and share meals with him. Among the four evangelists, Luke and John emphatically affirm the reality of Jesus' risen body. Luke narrates Jesus' appearances to his disciples, who thought he was a ghost, and reports Jesus saying: "Look at my hands and my feet, that it is I myself. Touch and see, because a ghost does not have flesh and bones as you can see I have" (Lk 24:39). Luke then reports that Jesus ate a piece of baked fish. John has the "doubting" Thomas put his fingers into Jesus' hands and his hand into Jesus' side to prove the reality of Jesus' body (Jn 20:27). In a later apparition by the Sea of Tiberias to seven disciples, including Peter, Jesus prepared a charcoal fire with bread and fish on it and invited them to eat breakfast with him (Jn 21:9-14).

While the reality of Jesus' risen body must be affirmed, at the same time we need to be careful not to think that Jesus' risen body was an ordinary body, such as the one he had prior to his death, that needs to perform the usual evacuating functions after drinking and eating bread and the fish. The "flesh and bones" that Luke says he shows to his disciples, whatever their nature, cannot be the kind of flesh and bones that we now have; otherwise the disciples would not have thought him to be a ghost. Indeed, the Gospels testify to the fact that Jesus' body acquires new properties that no ordinary body has: No longer physically limited by space and time, Jesus could go through closed doors and appear wherever and whenever he wished. Clearly, there is continuity in discontinuity, identity in difference, indeed, more the latter than the former, between the earthly Jesus and the risen Jesus. Will our own risen bodies be identical yet fundamentally different from the bodies we currently have and will they acquire the same properties as those of Christ's?

The Resurrection of the Dead

This question naturally leads us to consider our own resurrection. In the Apostles' Creed, we profess the "resurrection of the body" and in Nicene Creed we say we look for the "resurrection of the dead." I have mentioned above that according to the Christian faith there is an intrinsic connection between the resurrection of Jesus and our own resurrection in the sense that the former is the cause and the model of the latter. In other words, we will be raised from the dead because Jesus has been raised from the dead, and the way Jesus is alive in his new body is also the way we will be alive in our resurrected bodies. This is the point Paul makes in his letter to the Romans:

> Do you not know that all of us who have been baptized into Christ Jesus were baptized into his death? Therefore we have been buried with him by baptism into death, so that, just as Christ was raised from the dead by the glory of the Father, so we too might walk in newness of life.... If we have died with Christ, we believe we will also live with him. We know that Christ, being raised from the dead, will never die again; death no longer has dominion over him. The death he died, he died to sin, once for all; but the life he lives, he lives to God. So you also must consider

yourselves dead to sin and alive to God in Christ Jesus.
(Rom 6:3-11).

For Paul, the resurrection of Jesus is God's act: "God raised him
from the dead" (Rom 10:9). (This divine agency is often expressed
by means of the so-called divine passive: Jesus "was raised.") Paul
explicitly affirms that just as Jesus' resurrection is a deed of God's
creative power, so will be ours: "God raised the Lord and will also
us by his power" (1 Cor 6:14).

Here Paul expresses in a nutshell what the resurrected life is. It
is made possible by the death and resurrection of Jesus. It begins
in baptism and reaches its fullness in the resurrection from the
dead. Furthermore, whatever bodily condition Jesus is in now in
his risen state will also be ours in our resurrected state. This explanation sounds simple enough, but apparently it did not satisfy the Christians in Corinth. In their letter to Paul, which is now
missing, they asked Paul the million-dollar question: "How are the
dead raised? With what kind of body do they come?" (1 Cor 15:35).
Clearly, Paul is irritated by the question, and resorts to abuse by
calling the questioner "fool"—a procedure decidedly to be avoided
by professors if they want to get a favorable rating by the students
and receive tenure.

In his answer Paul makes use of three analogies taken from agri-
culture, biology, and astronomy, to use our modern terms. First,
each seed produces its own tree; secondly, each earthly animal has
its own body; and thirdly, each heavenly being (the sun, the moon,
and the star) possesses its own glory. Then Paul goes on to say: "So
it is with the resurrection of the dead. What is sown is perishable,
what is raised is imperishable. It is sown in dishonor, it is raised
in glory. It is sown in weakness, it is raised in power. It is sown a
physical body, it is raised a spiritual body" (1 Cor 15:42-44). What
Paul is saying is that there is some continuity between the body
we now have and the body that will be resurrected, similar to that
between what is sown (the seed/the physical body) and what has
grown from the seed (the tree/the spiritual body).

There is however more difference and discontinuity between the pre-resurrection body and the resurrected body, and Paul characterizes the difference by means of four couplets: (1) perishable--imperishable, (2) dishonor--glory, (3) weakness--power, and (4) physical--spiritual. He goes on to say that the first set of characteristics in these four pairs—perishability, dishonor, weakness, and physicality—belongs to the first, earthly Adam; and the second set—imperishability, glory, power, and spirituality—belongs to the last, heavenly Adam. Paul further says that the resurrection of the dead is not the result of human achievement but the work of God: "Flesh and blood cannot inherit the kingdom of God, nor does the perishable inherit the imperishable" (1 Cor 15:50).

We have no record as to whether the Corinthian Christians were satisfied with Paul's answer, but there is no doubt that modern readers will want to question him further about the identity between the pre-resurrection body and the resurrected body. I have mentioned above, in connection with the body of the risen Jesus, that it is more different from, though somehow identical with, the body he had when he was still alive. Before discussing the identity between the two bodies and the identity of the person before death and after resurrection, there is the prior question of the very possibility of resurrection itself.

First, as to the possibility of the resurrection, there should be no problem with it for those who believe in God's omnipotence. According to the New Testament, resurrection is an act of God's creative power. It is God who raises Jesus as well as all the dead. Since God is omnipotent, there should be in principle no obstacle to God's reconstituting the dead person from what that person has been and has done. Indeed, it may be argued that God's first act of creation is harder, if such a language can be used, than the reconstituting of the dead person since the former is done from nothing (*ex nihilo*), with no pre-existing material.

Secondly, with regard to the identity of the person before death and after the resurrection, it seems that some kind of continuity between the pre-resurrection body and the risen body is required.

Paul, as we have seen above, postulates some kind of identity between the seed (the former) and the tree (the latter) that grows out of that seed. The question then turns on how God's creative power brings about the resurrection. If God creates an entirely new body for, say, Peter Phan, then there does not seem to be an identity between the Peter before his death and the resurrected Peter. If God makes use of Peter's former body, or at least parts of it, to resurrect Peter, then it may be pointed out that Peter's former body, and even parts of it, no longer exists, especially if the resurrection occurs billions of years after Peter's death. Still it could be argued, as alluded to above, that God's omnipotence and omniscience can overcome the apparently impossible task of reassembling Peter's body, no matter how far and how long its parts have been dispersed or destroyed.

There are however two difficulties against this answer. First, in what has been called the "cannibalism case," suppose that Peter was drowned, his body was eaten by a shark, and the shark was consumed by a man, and this man was cannibalized by another man, and this man by yet another man (and the food chain can go on and on). Obviously Peter's body is an essential part of the shark, the man who eats the shark, and the man who eats the man who has eaten the shark, and the man who eats the man who has eaten the man who has eaten the shark. Which bodily part or parts belongs to Peter and which belongs to the shark and all the other men, which God presumably has to reassemble to resurrect Peter's body? Interestingly, already in the fifth century, Saint Augustine entertained this "cannibalism case" and suggested that the parts belong to the body in which they first appear, but his solution is far from fair to the shark and the other men. The second difficulty comes from modern cosmology, according to which the entire cosmos will either "freeze" by an absolute cold in eternal expansion or "fry" by a collapse into an absolute heat. In either scenario there is nothing left from which God can reassemble the bodies to resurrect them.

These two difficulties may exercise modern defenders of the resurrection but I doubt that they would bother Paul at all, not simply because cannibalism and contemporary cosmologies were beyond his ken. Rather it is because he has a personal experience of the risen Christ and because he is convinced that thanks to what Jesus has done for us, God will do for us what he has done for Christ. For Paul, Christ is "the first fruits of those who have fallen asleep" (1 Cor 15:20). Consequently, though all will be brought to life after death, each one will be raised "in proper order: Christ, the first fruits; then, at his coming, those who belong to Christ" (1 Cor 15:23). Christ is therefore "the firstborn among many brothers" (Rom 8:29), the "firstborn from the dead" (Col 1:18), "the first to rise from the dead" (Acts 26:23), and "the author of life" (Acts 3:15). Ultimately, for Paul, the resurrection is possible and will happen, not because we can prove it rationally, though, as we have seen above, he gallantly attempts to do so through various analogies, but because of the power of God who has shown his power and might in raising Jesus from the dead and establishing him in glory and who will do the same for us.

These answers may not be persuasive to those who insist on empirically verifiable evidence for the resurrection of the dead and hence will inevitably find Paul's various metaphors for the resurrection more obfuscating than illuminating. Indeed, what is the nature of "spiritual body"? Does it not sound like an oxymoron? The God who reconstitutes the various long-lost parts of the body to resurrect the person looks suspiciously more like a *deus ex machina* to bring about a happy ending to the Christian story than the God who respects the workings of the laws of nature.

To help understand the Pauline language about the resurrection of the dead, I would like to return once more to what I have said in the first chapter about the kind of language that is used in the Bible to talk about eternal life, in this case, the resurrection of the dead, and the need to interpret it very carefully. There I quoted the famous passage from Paul's First Letter to the Thessalonians (4:15-17) in which Paul speaks of the archangel's call, the sound of God's trumpet, Christ's descent to earth from heaven, the resurrection of those who have died in Christ, then the meeting in the air with Christ by those who will still be alive. I noted that this literature is apocalyptic, not descriptive or reportorial, and must neither be taken literalistically as historical report nor dismissed as mere mythology. A fundamentalistic reading would go to great lengths to chart the exact sequence of the events between Christ's descent from heaven to the "rapture" of the faithful and their meeting with Christ in the air. Perhaps an attempt will be made to correlate these events with those described in Revelation, especially in its last two chapters (21-22). It is highly unlikely however that a consensus will be reached with regard to the events themselves and their sequence, since there is a wide divergence among these apocalyptic texts. On the other hand, an equally literalistic but skeptical reading of these texts will dismiss them out of court as little more than science fiction and therefore misses their transformative message for our life.

In accord with my proposal that we discern the worlds *behind, of,* and *in front of* the biblical text, I suggest that we distinguish between what Paul says and what he means. What he *says* is couched in the stock-in-trade imagery of apocalyptic literature of which, as we have seen in the last chapter, Jesus himself makes frequent and liberal use: the voice of the archangel, the sound of the trumpet, the instantaneous transformation of the dead and of the living, rapture, flight into the air, meeting the Lord in the clouds, the struggle between heaven and earth, the destruction of this world, and the coming of a new heaven and a new earth, and so on. What Paul *means* must be discovered not beyond but in and through these images. Paul is not giving us an anticipatory report of what will transpire at the end of time. He is not trying to satisfy our curiosity about when and how the resurrection will take place, the various events preceding and following it, and the kind of bodies we will have. Rather, Paul is projecting into the end-time, which he thought would come in his lifetime, the resurrection of Jesus, of which he is absolutely certain because he has experientially encountered the risen Christ, and tries to spell out the consequences of this event for our present life and our own future resurrection from the dead.

First, the world *behind* the New Testament texts on the resurrection of the dead is the apocalyptic world with its deep conviction about the ultimate vindication of God's faithful ones (here, those who have died in Christ) and the total defeat of God's enemies, including sin and death. This apocalyptic worldview is of a piece with the Jewish apocalypticism from the third century B.C., as expressed by the authors of Daniel and various pseudepigrapha or apocrypha (writings that claimed to be inspired but are not included in the Bible). Apocalypticists view the community of believers as a minority whose survival is constantly threatened by its enemies, political and religious, because of its confession of faith and fidelity to the Covenant. They urge their fellow believers to remain faithful and patient, especially during the end time, when they have to struggle not only against hostile humans but also against demons and angels. And, for apocalypticists, there is no stronger means to sustain and encourage the faithful during times of trial and persecution than the hope in the resurrection. The resurrection of the dead is part of a series of events in which God intervenes in history to bring evil and evil people to an end and exercises the last judgment upon all humanity, after which the wicked will be condemned to eternal flames and the righteous will be vindicated and enter the kingdom of God. Then is inaugurated the new "aeon" (age) or the "aeon of aeons," in which the first paradise returns in a perfect form.

Apocalypticism, with its doctrines of the resurrection, the final judgment, and the coming of the aeon of aeons, is explicitly affirmed in the New Testament by John the Baptist who preaches repentance and imminent judgment. Jesus himself is an apocalyptist proclaiming the imminent coming of the kingdom of God, together with the resurrection of the dead and universal judgment. Moreover, by his various miracles, in particular by casting out demons, by forgiving sins, and in his vision of Satan falling from heaven (Lk 10:18) Jesus shows that the new aeon of the kingdom of God is already inaugurated in his message, actions, and person. The apocalyptic view is expressed in all the four gospels, in many letters of Paul, and above all, in the last book of the Bible, Revelation. In brief, this apocalyptic world lies *behind* all the New Testament passages affirming the resurrection of the dead, the historical context within which they must be interpreted in order to be correctly understood.

The world *of* the text is constituted by the actions of God the Father, who raised Jesus from the dead and will raise us from the dead in the same manner because of Jesus, together with Christ as Lord and Judge, and the Spirit, who will be as it were the soul or power by which our resurrected bodies will live (Paul's "spiritual body," that is animated by the Spirit). This world is the world of God's grace, mercy, and love which is given to all, Jews and Gentiles, free persons and slaves, women and men, without any distinction. It is the world in which salvation concerns the whole person, "soul" and "body" equally, in which diseases are healed and sins are forgiven, so that the resurrection of the "body" means the resurrection of the entire person, soul and body in their indissoluble unity. Hence, it is the world in which our lives are reflected as in a mirror; there we can see our faces in the deaf and the dumb, the lepers and the lame, the sick and the poor, the tax-collectors and the prostitutes, the possessed and the demons, the Pharisees and the Sadducees, Pilate and Herod, Satan and Beelzebul, and those who have been brought back from the dead like the young man in Nain, the daughter of Jairus, and Lazarus. To all of these as well as to all of us, none excluded, even those we consider evil and lost, God has offered salvation because there is no limit to God's all-embracing love. Our hope for salvation and the resurrection must likewise be limitless and all-embracing, otherwise it is unworthy of God.

The world *in front of* the text is the world of vigilance and hope into which Paul invites the Thessalonian and Corinthian Christians, and by implication, all of us, to enter, the world sustained by Christ's promised return, and animated by the power of the Spirit, the world in which we are called to "console one another" with the hope of the resurrection (1 Thess 4:18). Paul points out that if what we Christians hope for is only this world and not the resurrection of the dead, "we are of all people most to be pitied" (1 Cor 15:19). Again, he says: "If the dead are not raised, "let us eat and drink, for tomorrow we die" (1 Cor 15:32). The world *in front of* the text moves us beyond consumerism, materialism, and despair. It beckons us to taste a joy that lasts longer than foods and drinks, and to live a life worthy of our eternal worth and dignity. The resurrection of the dead, then, is no pie in the sky, much less the opium for the masses, but a call and incentive to work together, believers of all religions and unbelievers, for a better world for us and the generations that follow us, for it is *in* and not *from* this world that we are saved, and it is our *physical* bodies and not bloodless ghosts that will be resurrected.

9

JESUS' RETURN IN GLORY

WHEN AND HOW?

Christians profess in the Nicene Creed that Christ, who has ascended into heaven and is seated at the right hand of the Father, will come again in glory to judge the living and the dead and that his kingdom will have no end. This affirmation of the Creed is couched in heavily symbolic language, from "ascension into heaven" to "sitting at the right hand of the Father" to "come again to judge the living and the dead." Of course, if these metaphors are taken literally, skeptics will have a field day with tongue-in-cheek questions such as: How did Christ fly up to heaven? In a golden chariot or a supersonic airplane? Does God the Father have hands? If Christ sits on his right hand, who sits on his left? The Holy Spirit? What kind of chair or throne do they sit on? How long will they be seated? In what vehicle will Christ come down to earth again? In a helicopter perhaps? Where will Christ's judgment of the living and the dead take place? Is there a stadium large enough to hold all humans who have ever lived? Will the judgment be carried out as Michelangelo depicts it in his fresco on the wall of the Sistine Chapel, or as Giotto in the Arena Chapel, or as Fra Angelico, or Jheronimus Bosch, or Hans Memling on their triptychs? Literally-minded Christians will of course brush aside these questions as manifestations of a lack of faith and go on reciting the Creed as if it describes the heavenly state of affairs.

No doubt, modern readers, touting their scientific knowledge, will purse their mouths in a self-satisfied smirk and dismiss these statements of the Creed as a relic of the ancient triple-decker cosmology. Yet, ironically, it is they, more than their medieval counterparts, that were more alarmed by the approach of the end of the world, as people old enough to remember the year 2000 can testify. As the fateful New Year's Day passed with nary a cosmic cataclysm, and as the apocalyptic hullabaloo and New Year's Eve revelries faded, the general awareness of Jesus' return in glory, which is often associated with the end of the world, like the tidal wave, also receded. This happened even among fundamentalist Christians who firmly hold the belief that a period of a thousand years will occur first after which Christ will come (postmillennialism), or that Christ will come first and then there will be a millennium of peace (premillennialism). This eclipse of the consciousness of Christ's future return in glory to judge the whole humanity is spiritually detrimental not only for Evangelicals but also for mainline Christians. It dims their hope in the final victory of God, the rule of Jesus as the cosmic Lord, and the transforming power of the Holy Spirit. Fortunately, this hope is confidently affirmed in every celebration of the Eucharist where it is proclaimed: "Christ has died, Christ is risen, Christ will come again."

To recover this Christian hope in the second coming of Christ and his universal lordship, I first consider what the New Testament says about Jesus' future return in glory to judge the living and the dead. Next I show how the belief in the return of Christ affects the everyday Christian life. Last, I will relate this doctrine of Christ the universal judge to the Catholic belief in purgatory.

Jesus' Return in Glory

The word "return" in the phrase "Jesus' return/coming again in glory/second coming" is *parousia* in Greek. It is used to refer to Christ's expected return in glory at the end of time. It is not used to refer to Christ's first coming on earth in the incarnation, because he then came in humility and not in glory. The common expression "second coming" is not used in the New Testament, though we read in Heb 9:28: "Christ ... will appear a second time." At times the word *epiphaneia*, meaning manifestation, is used instead of *parousia* (2 Thess 2:8; 1 Tim 6:14; 2 Tim 4:1, 8; Titus 2:13). Lastly, *apocalypsis*, meaning uncovering or revelation, is also used sometimes in the same sense as *parousia*.

Christ's second coming in glory is often connected with the Old Testament's notion of the "day of Yahweh," the coming of which was announced by the prophets as a day of both salvation and judgment. In apocalyptic literature the day of Yahweh is presented as the day of destruction of God's enemies and vindication for God's faithful people. In the New Testament, this expected day of Yahweh is proclaimed to have arrived with the life and ministry of Jesus; in his person the end-time, which is associated with day of Yahweh, and signified by the coming of the kingdom of God, has been inaugurated. After Jesus' resurrection and ascension, two men in white robes asked the disciples: "Men of Galilee, why do you stand looking up toward heaven? This Jesus, who has been taken up from you into heaven, will come in the same way as you saw him go into heaven" (Acts 1:11).

The earliest expression of the Christian faith in the parousia of Christ is found in the two letters of Paul which we have seen in the last chapters, namely 1 Thess 4:13-17 and 1 Cor 15:23-28; 50-52. Here I will examine another Pauline text, 2 Thess 2:1-12. One of the purposes of this letter is to address one possible misunderstanding of Paul's teaching about the "day of the Lord." In his first letter to the Thessalonian Christians Paul had assured them that the day of the Lord would be coming soon, perhaps in his and their lifetime

(1 Thess 4:17). As time passed, the Thessalonians began wondering whether Paul's prediction about Christ's imminent return in glory is incorrect. In his second letter, Paul attempts to deal with this faith crisis, first, by reaffirming the belief in Christ's parousia against those who deny it, and second, by stating that it has not yet arrived, as some Thessalonians with overheated eschatological imagination claim.

In vivid language drawn from the Old Testament apocalyptic literature, Paul warns those who deny Christ's parousia that they will be punished "when the Lord Jesus is revealed from heaven with his mighty angels, in flaming fire." They will "suffer the punishment of eternal ruin, separated from the presence of the Lord and from the glory of his might, when he comes to be glorified among his saints and to be marveled at on that day among all who have believed" (2 Thess 1:7-10). On the other hand, while condemning those denying the parousia, Paul also chides those Thessalonians who, perhaps invoking his teaching and with an overheated eschatological imagination, were alarming their fellow believers with talks affirming that "the day of the Lord is already here" (2 Thess 2:2). Paul argues that certain signs would precede Christ's parousia but were not yet at hand. He affirms that "that day will not come unless the rebellion comes first and the lawless one is revealed, the one destined for destruction. He opposes and exalts himself above every so-called god or object of worship so that he takes his seat in the temple of God, declaring himself to be God" (2 Thess 2:3-4). Who this "lawless one," is whose terrible sin of blasphemy must precede Christ's parousia, Paul does not specify. He does however say that "the coming of the lawless one is apparent in the working of Satan" (2 Thess 2:9) and that "the mystery of lawlessness" is already at work in the world, but his action is limited because he is being restrained by someone whose identity, Paul says, is already known to the Thessalonian Christians. When this restraining person is removed, then the "lawless one" will be revealed, whom, Paul adds, "the Lord Jesus will destroy with the breath of his mouth, annihilating him by the manifestation of his coming" (2 Thess 2:8).

I am sure that readers would pester Paul for more specific information on the identity of the "lawless one" (is he Satan himself?) and of the person who is now restraining the lawless one (is he Jesus himself?) and the signs and especially the precise date of Jesus' parousia. Like any good apocalypticist, Paul will certainly not specify the day and the time. He will repeat to us what he wrote to the Thessalonians: "Now concerning the times and the seasons, brothers and sisters, you do not need to have anything written to you. For you yourselves know very well that the day of the Lord will come like a thief in the night.... So then let us not fall asleep as others do, but let us keep awake and be sober" (1 Cor 5:1-6). Paul is not into prognosticating the time of the second coming of Jesus; he is only interested in urging us "not to fall asleep" and to "keep awake and be sober" so that we will not be caught unprepared for Jesus' coming.

Curiosity about the end-time had already haunted Jesus' disciples themselves who asked him: "Tell us, when will this happen, and what sign will there be of your coming, and of the end of the age?" (Mt 24:3). To this question Jesus contented himself with giving apocalyptic stock-in-trade signs and urged his disciples to be vigilant: "Therefore, stay awake! For you do not know on which day your Lord will come" (Mt 24:42). This spiritual exhortation for vigilance has not of course deterred inquiring minds from wanting to know the precise date of Jesus' glorious return. They will no doubt mine the New Testament for clues, and of clues there are plenty in Jesus' discourses on the end-time contained in Matthew 24; Mark 13 and Luke 21, often called the Olivet Discourse, because they allegedly took place on Mount of Olives. Let's cite a few of them: false messiahs, global warfare, natural disasters, persecutions of Christians, increase in evil, worldwide preaching of the Gospel, sins of blasphemy, the day of great tribulation, and above all, cosmic cataclysms: "The sun will be darkened, and the moon will not give its light, and the stars will fall from the sky, and the powers in heaven will be shaken, and then the sign of the Son of Man will appear in heaven, and all the tribes of the earth will mourn, and they will see the Son of Man coming upon the clouds of heaven with power and great glory. And he will send out his angels with a trumpet blast, and they will gather his elect from the four winds, from one end of the heavens to the other" (Mt 14:29-31).

Following this script, Hollywood movie producers, with fantastic special effects at their disposal, would make a humongous profit with films on the end-time that will leave the pyrotechnics of Harry Potter movies in the dust. Unfortunately, these films, while titillating our imagination, will have nothing true or meaningful to say about the end-time and Jesus' parousia. The reason for this is simple: The eschatological discourses are a grab bag of apocalyptic imagery that should not be taken as a blow-by-blow description of the end-time scenario. Rather they are merely literary devices to underline the urgency and seriousness of the decision for God and Jesus here and now. Consequently we must resist all attempts at identifying any of these signs with a particular historical event or natural disaster.

The same thing should be said of the "antichrist" who is said to appear at the end-time. The expression *antichristos* is found only in the letters of John (1 Jn 2:18, 22; 4:3; 2 Jn 7), with *anti* meaning opposing. The antichrist is thus someone fighting against Christ. He is perhaps the equivalent of Paul's "the lawless one." John warns his community of the presence of the many antichrists among them: "Children, it is the last hour; and just as you heard that the antichrist was coming, so now many antichrists have appeared" (1 Jn 2:18). The defining feature of the antichrist is denial of the Father and of the Son (1 Jn 2:22), and more precisely, denial of "Jesus Christ as coming in the flesh" (2 Jn 7), which is the sum total of all oppositions to Christ. Again, the antichrist is the apocalyptic symbol of all the forces, personal and impersonal, fighting against Christ and his followers and should not be identified with any specific historical person.

Jesus as the Universal Judge

If there is anything about the end-time and the parousia on which there is universal agreement, it is that Jesus will sit in judgment over the whole humanity. This is what the Creed professes: Christ will come again "to judge the living and the dead." This judgment is commonly called the "final/general judgment," to distinguish it from the "particular/personal judgment," which each of us is said to undergo immediately after our death, following which we immediately go to heaven, hell, or, as we shall see shortly, purgatory.

The belief that Jesus will judge the whole world at the parousia is rooted in the Old Testament conviction that God will judge Israel and the nations. The prophets never tired of proclaiming that Yahweh is the king who will judge his chosen people and the whole world on the "day of Yahweh." This divine judgment is presented in various images: God as the shepherd sorting out the good and the bad among his flock (Ezek 34:17-22), as the harvester of grain and olives (Isa 17:5-6), as the winepress of wrath (Isa 63:1-6), and as the owner of a furnace for smelting and purifying (Ezek 22:18-22). The highpoint of God's judgment is described in Daniel 7, where the reign of God dawns and destroys all kingdoms opposed to God. It is important to note that even in the Old Testament the ultimate purpose of divine judgment is not to punish but to arouse conversion and hope in the sinners. God's wrath against his people is always accompanied by God's loving mercy and will to save them.

In the New Testament, the message about God's final and definitive judgment, which will be exercised through God's Messiah, is proclaimed by John the Baptist (Mt 3:10-12). In addition, John performed the baptism of repentance by water for those who wanted to escape the coming judgment (Mt 3:5-11). Jesus himself often speaks of the judgment on the last day and the "day of judgment." In his parables and other sayings, Jesus urges his hearers to accept his teaching and repent in order to avoid condemnation and enter the kingdom of God. Jesus declares that he himself will appear as the judge of all, so that the Old Testament "day of Yahweh" and the "day of Judgment" has become the "day of the Lord" (1 Cor 1:8; 1 Thess 5:2; Heb 1). According to John, the Father has established Jesus as judge on the last day (Jn 5:26-30). Indeed, the judgment has already taken place here and now, as the person who refuses to believe in Jesus is already judged and condemned (Jn 3:18). As with Yahweh in the Old Testament, Jesus as the universal judge does not come to condemn but to save the world: "For God did not send his Son into the world to condemn the world, but to save the world through him" (Jn 3:17). Thus, the "day of the Lord" is the day of mercy, forgiveness, grace, and salvation.

The Day of Judgment and Christian Life

In popular imagination the day of judgment is closely associated with the end time, and because the end of the world is still billions of years away, most people are generally not too worried about it. It is not unlike our consciousness of our own mortality. Occasionally we are brought face to face with it, as when we attend a funeral, but soon we banish the thought of our own death out of our mind and carry on with living as if death will never knock on our door, or at least not anytime soon, as if dying were not something occurring at every moment of our life.

But as dying is a continuous and constant process, so is Christ's judgment. Jesus' parable on the last judgment in Mt 25:31-46 makes it clear that we are being judged every single day, and in a way we least expect. The parable introduces the judgment of the nations with a majestic scene: "When the Son of Man comes in his glory, and all the angels with him, he will sit upon his glorious throne, and all the nations will be assembled before him. And he will separate them one from another, as a shepherd separates the sheep from the goats" (Mt 25:31-32). Jesus then pronounces the sentence on both the good and the bad people. To the former he says: "Come, you who are blessed by my Father. Inherit the kingdom prepared for you from the foundation of the world" (Mt 25:34); and to the latter: "Depart from me, you accursed, into the eternal fire prepared for the devil and his angels" (Mt 25:41).

Both groups are shocked by the criteria Jesus uses for his judgment, that is, whether they have or have not fed him when he was hungry, given him drink when he was thirsty, welcomed him when he was a stranger, clothed him when he was naked, cared for him when he was ill, and visited him when he was in prison. Both groups protest that they have never done those things to Jesus. Then comes Jesus' astounding reply: whatever they did or failed to do for the least ones among them, they did or failed to do for him personally. The last judgment then is a daily judgment, pronounced on us when we do or fail to do these most common things to the most marginalized people among us, the least of Jesus' brothers and sisters, with whom Jesus identifies himself.

Personal Purification or Purgatory?

The view of the final judgment as an ongoing process here and now, and not just an act that will take place at the end of the world, is an appropriate place to approach the Catholic doctrine of purgatory. *Catechism of the Catholic Church* defines "purgatory" as the process of purification that a person who dies in God's grace and friendship has to undergo immediately after death "so as to achieve the holiness necessary to enter the joy of heaven" (§1030). While such purification is necessary, the frequent focus on the postmortem "duration" of this process on the other world as well as on the "location" of the purgatory is misplaced and highly problematic, especially when it is thought that the intercessory prayer of the church and the application of Mass intentions, indulgences, and one's own merits to the souls in purgatory can somehow alleviate their pains and shorten the length of their stay in purgatory.

Furthermore, when purgatory is conceived of as the soul's undergoing "purifying punishments" in the other world to complete the "payment" of the temporal "penalty" due to sins (as distinct from the "guilt," which has been forgiven), as this was commonly done in Latin theology, the "purifying punishments" risk to be wrongly understood as *additional* penalty which God further imposes on the souls in purgatory but which by definition they can do nothing by themselves to satisfy since they are now beyond the time of doing good works and earning merits.

In view of these well-nigh insoluble difficulties, just as it is more helpful to understand the last judgment as a process occurring *here and now* in each of our moral decision, so it is better to understand "purgatory," as the theologian Karl Rahner suggests, as a constant process of full psychological and spiritual integration, often quite painful and lengthy, of the various levels of our personality into our fundamental option of love for God. Purgatory then is not an additional punishment imposed externally by God after death on the souls already in peace with God but still are burdened with parts of the temporal punishments due to their sins left uncompleted. Rather it is something we do *here and now*, every day, to achieve full communion with God and with our sisters and brothers, a painful yet joyful work, for which we need the prayers and support of the whole community.

In conclusion, the events we tend to project into the distant future, at the end of time, such as the final judgment and purgation, which we can banish from our everyday life, turn out to be very close, indeed, present to us at every moment of our life and of decisive relevance. Thus, despite its etymological meaning, eschatology does not deal with the "last things," but with the "present things," matters that are of utmost importance for us here and now, and of course, also there and then. Thus, the Christian hope for the second coming of Christ in glory is not at all a passive, much less idle, waiting for Jesus, with hands joined and eye turned toward heaven. On the contrary, this "hope" and "waiting"—the double meaning of the Spanish *esperar*—for the coming of Christ in glory demand an active engagement in the work of *tikkun olam* [repairing/healing the world], as the Jewish tradition puts it. This work of building a peaceful and just society is done through the ethical and ritual observance of the *mitzvot*—commandments or religious obligations—and, according to the Jewish belief, will hasten the coming of the messiah and the messianic age. For Christians, of course, the messiah has already come in Jesus, but he will come *again* in glory to judge the living and the dead and to reign as the cosmic lord.

Thus, using the fantastic imagery of apocalypticism to describe the imminent return of Jesus in glory and his judgment of the living and the dead, the New Testament does not lead us away from the Earth but rather demands a deeper and stronger commitment to it, repairing and healing the world to make it more just and peaceful, and thus a fitting home for the Lord of the universe and the resurrected and transformed humanity.

10

THE EUCHARIST

A FORETASTE OF ETERNAL LIFE?

In the last chapter I have noted that Christians are daily reminded in the Eucharist of the future return of Christ in glory when they proclaim after the consecration of the bread and the wine: "Christ has died, Christ is risen, Christ will come again." But the Eucharist does not merely proclaim that Christ will come again; rather, it "re-presents," that is, makes *present* this future coming of Jesus here and now for the assembly. Consequently, there is no better way to counteract the tendency to relegate the so-called "Last Things" into the distant and indefinite future and banish them from our consciousness than to reflect on the deep connections between the Eucharist and all the eschatological realities we have dealt with so far, from death and dying to heaven, hell, resurrection, the parousia, and the universal judgment.

In this way the main goal of this book will be achieved, that is, spelling out the practical implications of the Last Things for our daily living, and not merely satisfying our intellectual curiosity about the mysteries of the afterlife. It will become clear that *living into death is truly dying into life.*

The Eucharist is known by many different names, each highlighting a particular aspect of this sacrament. Among Catholics it is commonly called the (Holy) Mass and has been declared by Vatican II's Constitution on the Sacred Liturgy to be "the source and summit of the Christian life" (§11). *Catechism of the Catholic Church* speaks of the Eucharist as thanksgiving and praise to God the Father; as the memorial of the sacrifice of Christ on the cross; as the sacrifice offered by the whole church on earth, in heaven and in purgatory; as the embodiment of Christ's presence in his word, the priest, the bread and wine, and the assembly; and as a meal in which the faithful partake in the body and blood of Christ and enter in communion with Christ and one another (see §§1356-1401). I will not discuss these three aspects of the Eucharist—thanksgiving, sacrifice, and meal—as such; rather I will consider how in the Eucharist, in the words of Saint Thomas Aquinas, "a pledge of the life to come is given to us." In other words, I will focus on the eschatological dimension of the Eucharist. As the first step, we consider what Jesus intends to do during the Last Supper.

What Did Jesus Do at the Last Supper?

The Eucharist takes its origins in the Last Supper that Jesus shares with his disciples. It is called "Last" because it was the meal Jesus ate before his death on the cross the following day. But it was also the "last" in the series of innumerable meals Jesus had eaten during his life, especially during his public ministry. To understand the significance of Jesus' sharing meals with others, a practice which is often referred to as "table fellowship," it is useful to remember that during Jesus' time, there was a strong insistence among the Sadducees, and especially the Pharisees, on eating only with persons who had "undefiled hands" (Mk 7:2-4), that is, people who are in a state of ritual purity. Meals were therefore rituals where gender distinction, racial and ethnic differences, economic rank, social class, political power, and religious boundaries were reinforced.

Jesus rejects this exclusionary practice in eating meals. He welcomes to his table and eats with anyone, men and women, rich and poor, pure and impure, good and bad, Jews and Gentiles. He is aware that because of his practice of radically open table fellowship, he is accused by his enemies of being "a glutton and a drunkard, a friend of tax collectors and sinners" (Mt 11:19). Of the four evangelists, Luke emphasizes most strongly Jesus' practice of radical inclusiveness in eating with the people his society regards as impure and sinful. The Pharisees and the scribes repeatedly accuse him of "receiving sinners and eating with them" (Lk 15:1-2). But Jesus also eats in the homes of several Pharisees, and it is on one of these occasions that a woman, who is a well-known sinner in town, anoints Jesus' feet (Lk 7:36-50).

On the duty to practice all-inclusive hospitality, Jesus' instruction is quite explicit: "When you give a luncheon or a dinner, do not invite your friends or your brothers or your relatives or rich neighbors, in case they may invite you in return, and you will be repaid. But when you give a banquet, invite the poor, the cripples, the lame, and the blind. And you will be blessed, because they cannot repay you, for you will be repaid at the resurrection of the righteous" (Lk 14:12-14). In the parable of the great banquet, after the invited guests decline to come, the owner of the house tells the servants: "Go out at once into the streets and lanes of the town and bring in the poor, the crippled, the blind and the lame" (Lk 14:21). Clearly, open and all-inclusive table fellowship is intentionally used by Jesus as a root metaphor to announce the coming of the reign of God. Meals to which everyone, without any distinction whatsoever, is equally invited are symbols of the reconciliation between God and the whole humanity, and not only the people of Israel.

It is in this context that Jesus links the practice of inclusive table fellowship and the eschatological consummation: "Then people will come from east and west, from north and south, and will eat in the kingdom of God" (Lk 13:29). It is also in the context of Jesus' practice of inclusive table fellowship that the Last Supper should be understood. Of course, there is an added context, that is, the Passover meal, which must be taken into account to grasp what Jesus intends to do during the Last Supper. It is highly likely that Jesus celebrated his last meal as a Passover meal, but given the totally new meaning that he gave to the bread and the wine, the Last Supper was not just a Passover meal like any other. By pronouncing: "This is my body" over the bread and "This is my blood of the covenant poured out for many" over the cup of wine, Jesus imparted a new reality with a new meaning and a new purpose to this food and drink (which later Catholic doctrine calls "transubstantiation") and linked the Last Supper to his death on the cross the next day which he would undergo as a sacrificial death and thus established a new covenant for the forgiveness of sin.

Though the emphasis on the sacrificial nature of the Last Supper and the real presence of Jesus in the bread and the wine is legitimate, there is another dimension, no less important, which must be kept in mind, and that is its proclamation of the future return of Jesus and the eschatological banquet. Just as the Passover celebration is an anticipation of and longing for the final day when Israel would share in the messianic banquet (Isa 25:6-9; 53:13), so the Last Supper, celebrated in the framework of the Passover meal, anticipates and longs for Christ's return in glory and the messianic banquet, as Jesus is reported by the Synoptics to have declared: "I tell you, I will never again drink of the fruit of the vine until that day when I drink it new with you in my Father's kingdom." (Mt 26:29; Mk 14:25). Luke's version differs somewhat, as it reports Jesus' words at the beginning of the meal rather after the blessing of the cup, and makes Jesus refer to the Passover celebration as a whole and not simply to the wine: "I have eagerly desired to eat this Passover with you before I suffer; for I tell you, I will not eat it until it is fulfilled in the kingdom of God" (Lk 22:15-16).

Clearly, then, the Eucharist as both sacrifice and meal has an essential eschatological dimension. Paul understands this dimension well when he adds to his account of the Last Supper his own interpretation: "For as often as you eat this bread and drink this cup, you proclaim the Lord's death until he comes" (1 Cor 11:26). Thus the Eucharist is both a looking-back to Jesus' passion and death and a looking-forward to Jesus' future return in glory at the end of time. It is both a memorial of the Last Supper and an anticipation and a partial, albeit real, realization of the Eschatological Supper in which Jesus and all his followers will share together.

Here it is important to recall what is said above about Jesus' practice of all-inclusive table fellowship. It is unfortunate that popular imagination and artistic representations (think of Leonardo da Vinci's painting of the Last Supper) present only the Twelve sitting at the dinner table with Jesus and thus turn the Last Supper into an exclusive club of elite males. Where are, we may ask, "the poor, the cripples, the lame, and the blind" whom Jesus commands us to invite when we give a banquet? Where are the women who supported and accompanied him during his ministry? Where are the children whom he blessed and held out as models of discipleship to enter the kingdom of God? Unless we practice in the celebration of the Eucharist the all-inclusive table fellowship that Jesus practiced, abolishing all forms of separation and discrimination based on gender, ethnicity, race, economics, class, and religious distinction, we are not proclaiming the death of Jesus, as Paul puts it, "until he comes," whether we celebrate the Mass according to Pope Paul VI's *Novus Ordo* or in the Tridentine rite in Latin.

Transubstantiation of Bread and Wine or the Personal Presence of Jesus?

There is another way in which the Eucharist foreshadows and actualizes the final transformation of humanity and the world, and that is in the change of the bread and the wine into the body and the blood of Christ. As we have seen above, during the Last Supper, Jesus pronounces the words: "This is my body" over the bread, and "This is my blood of the covenant" (Matthew and Mark), or "The new covenant in my blood" (Luke and Paul) over the wine. It is believed that with these words Jesus identifies himself with these realities of bread and wine and that therefore he is really and truly present in them, in his body and blood.

This "Real Presence" was explained in an overly-realistic way by Paschasius Radbertus, a ninth-century monk, who maintains that the Jesus present in the consecrated bread and wine is the flesh born of Mary, which has suffered on the Cross and risen again, and which is miraculously multiplied by God at each consecration. Radbertus's physicalist understanding of the Real Presence was sharply attacked by his fellow monk Ratramnus, who proposes a more spiritual notion of the Real Presence, according to which the consecrated bread and wine serve simply as "figures" to remind us of Jesus. Ratramnus's overly figurative view was later found to be incompatible with the Catholic teaching that the bread and the wine are changed into the body and blood of Christ and was condemned by Pope Leo IX in 1050. In 1079, the monk Berengar of Tours, who denied a substantial change of the bread and the wine into the body and blood of Christ in the Eucharist, was made to subscribe to the statement of the Council of Rome that "the bread and wine which are placed on the altar are, by the mystery of the sacred prayer and the words of the Redeemer, substantially changed into the true and proper and life-giving body and blood of Jesus Christ our Lord."

In the twelfth century Roland Bandinelli, later Pope Alexander III (d. 1181), introduced the term "transubstantiation" to designate the change of the bread and the wine into the body and blood of Christ. This term was adopted by the Fourth Lateran Council (1215) in its teaching on the Eucharist to refer to this substantial change.

Saint Thomas Aquinas gives a classic formulation to this doctrine by means of Aristotle's distinction between "substance" (what a thing is) and "accidents" (its qualifying properties). Thomas explains that the "substance" of the bread and the wine are "transubstantiated" into the substance of the body and blood of Christ, whereas their "accidents" (e.g., their taste and color) remain unchanged.

The issue of how to understand the presence of Christ in the Eucharist arose again during the Protestant Reformation in the sixteenth century. Luther holds that Jesus is really present in the Eucharist *together with* ("in, with, and under") the bread and the wine which remain unchanged. Hence, instead of "transubstantiation," he uses "consubstantiation" ("con" is the Latin *cum* meaning "with"). In contrast, the council of Trent in its decree on the Eucharist (1551) teaches that "by the consecration of the bread and wine there takes place a change of the whole substance of bread into the substance of the body of Christ our Lord and of the whole substance of wine into the substance of his blood. This change the holy Catholic Church has fittingly and properly names 'transubstantiation'."

The purpose of the preceding brief overview of the developments of the theology of the Real Presence is to argue that despite its positive contribution, the traditional theology of the presence of Jesus in the Eucharist in terms of "transubstantiation" needs correction in order to recover the neglected eschatological dimension of the Eucharist. One of strengths of the theory of transubstantiation is its explanation of how Jesus is made present in the bread and the wine. Through what has been called the "ontology of things," the transubstantiation theory explains well how material things such as bread and wine can become, as the council of Trent puts it, "truly, really, and substantially" the body and blood of Christ, that is, by being changed into another reality (the "substance" of Jesus' body and blood), without losing their external appearances (their "accidents" of bread and wine). The focus of the transubstantiation theology has been on the ontology of "things": the presence of Jesus' body and blood in the "things" of bread and wine, and conversely, the change of the "things" of bread and wine into the body and blood of Jesus. Questions then naturally arise as to whether the "body" of Jesus in the consecrated bread includes his bones, hair, skin, and other bodily parts, and in a similar way, whether his "blood" contains red and white cells, plasma, and other elements.

Because of its one-sided focus on bread, wine, body, and blood as "*things*," the transubstantiation theory woefully fails to express the *personal* nature of Jesus' presence in the Eucharist. The point of Jesus' sayings over the bread and the wine at the Last Supper is not to perform a miraculous transformation of these material things into his body and blood, understood as physical things. The miracle does not lie in Jesus' spectacular changing the "substance" of the bread and the wine into the "substance" of his body and blood, while leaving their "accidents" unchanged, so that the proper reaction would be to marvel at Jesus' awesome power to override the physical laws. Rather it consists in Jesus' real presence, in and through these material things, as *a person to other persons*, first to his disciples and then to all his future followers, despite his *real absence* during the long interval between his death and his return in glory. The only appropriate response to this kind of Jesus' presence-in-absence is both a loving abiding in his presence and *a deep longing during Jesus' absence for his full manifestation at the end of time*. This interpersonal "real presence-despite-physical-absence" or "physical-absence-in-real-presence" cannot be expressed by the "ontology of things" that undergirds the theory of transubstantiation. What is needed is an "ontology of persons," in which objects are transformed not by changing their "substance" or nature but by acquiring new meanings and new ends in the context of interpersonal relationships.

Thus, for instance, a rose, as a physical object, is but a flower. However, as a gift in a relationship of interpersonal love and as a symbol of this love, it acquires, while still remaining a flower, a new meaning and a new end in an interpersonal relationship, by which the giver of the rose is made personally present to its recipient and vice versa. This new meaning and this new end transforms the rose into a new reality, a "sign" and "instrument," or a sacrament, of the mutual love between the giver and the recipient of the rose. In this newly acquired nature, the rose is more intensely real than its botanical nature.

In a similar way, what happens to the bread and the wine in the Eucharist is that they acquire a new meaning ("transsignification") and a new end ("transfinalization"). Their new meaning is that they are now the "sign" and "instrument" of Jesus' abiding personal presence to his disciples and their presence to him, whereas their new "end" is that they are now the spiritual food and drink nourishing the Christian community as it waits in hope for the glorious return of its Lord. There is therefore a double dimension in the Eucharist: one the one hand, as sign and instrument, the bread and wine are the symbols of Jesus' *real presence* in and to the community. On the other hand, as end, they highlight Jesus' *real absence*, since in eating and drinking Jesus' body and blood, the community proclaims that Christ is still to come in glory. Real presence and real absence are the two constitutive dimensions of Christian eschatology. The kingdom of God is "already" (present) but "not yet" (absent). These two aspects of eschatology are not mutually contradictory; on the contrary, in the ongoing human history, they reinforce each other.

"Real Absence": In Anticipation of the Transformed World

It is in the "real absence" of Jesus in the Eucharist that its eschatological dimension becomes most apparent. On the one hand, as the bread and the wine are really changed into the body and blood of Christ, they already represent in anticipation what the whole cosmos will become at the end of time. At the offertory, the priest offers the bread to God saying that it is that "which earth has given and human hands have made." Similarly, he says of the wine that it is "fruit of the vine and work of human hands." Clearly, the bread and the wine are not seen as two self-standing and separate things but as symbols and representations of the whole material world and as the products of human work. In them the whole world—human and cosmic—are present. As they are transformed into the body and blood of Christ, so too are the whole cosmos and the entire humanity with all its achievements. What becomes the body and blood of Christ in the Eucharist is not just the bread and the wine but also, in and through them, the whole material world (the earth that gives the bread and the vine that produces the wine) and the entire humanity (the work of human hands that bake the bread and make the wine). And, as the bread and the wine become the body and blood of Christ without losing what makes them appear as bread and wine, so the material world and human labor are transformed into the body and blood of Christ without forfeiting what makes them be parts of the material world and human labor. Thus, if we want to know what will happen to the world and humanity at the end of time, the transubstantiation of the bread and the wine in the Eucharist gives a clue: real transformation but without loss of identity.

But, as I have argued above, in the Eucharist Christ, albeit really present, is also really absent. Because of this real absence, we may say that in the Eucharist Jesus is really present but not yet *totally* present. The *Christus totus* [the whole Christ], or the *Cosmic Christ*, composed of all his sisters and brothers and the whole material universe, is not yet present, here and now. Unfortunately, with the doctrine of transubstantiation there has been such a strong emphasis on the "real presence" of Jesus in the bread and the wine that his "real absence," and hence, eschatology, have been eclipsed. As a consequence we tend to forget that Jesus and God's kingdom are still to come, that Jesus is still to return, that the world awaits total transformation.

As the Eucharist is being celebrated and as we are well fed with Christ's body and blood, we run the risk of forgetting that there are still millions of people who go to bed with empty stomachs; millions of children are dying daily of easily preventable diseases; nations are being torn apart by war and violence; bombs are dropped on women and children; and the environment and natural resources are being destroyed by unrestrained greed and rampant consumerism. In this tragic situation, in the Eucharist we do not only praise God for all his great deeds in history, give thanks to God for all God's blessings, and are filled with joy as we make the ministry and the saving death of Christ on the cross present in our community ("transubstantiation"), but our hearts are also tinged by sadness and sorrow at the fact that the world is still steeped in brokenness and suffering, that we ourselves have contributed to this sinful condition, that our churches have been complicit in oppression and exploitation, that the kingdom of God is long in coming, in a word, that Jesus is still absent.

However, because of what God has done in and for Jesus, of which the Eucharist is a "memorial," because of Jesus' urging that in the midst of this not yet fully redeemed world we "take courage" since he has already "conquered the world." (Jn 16:3), and because of Jesus' promise that he will come back to bring us to his Father's house where there are many mansions (Jn 14:2-3), our sadness does not turn into despair but rather our hearts are suffused with hope. This hope is kept alive by a deep longing for what is still to come, the kind of aching desire we feel when separated from those we love dearly. We yearn to hear their voices, see their faces, embrace their bodies, and kiss and hold them. That is how mystics talk about their "sensations" of God, and in a similar way we hope and long for the day when we can sit at the heavenly banquet where we no longer need bread and wine to signify Jesus' presence since Jesus will no longer be absent but fully present.

But this longing for the future heavenly Eucharist is no idle or passive waiting. Christ's disciples who eat the bread of life and drink the cup of blessing in the Eucharist would make a mockery of the body and blood of Christ if they do nothing to feed the hungry, slake the thirsty, welcome the stranger, clothe the naked, heal the sick, visit the prisoners, because all these people are also "transubstantiated" into the body and blood of Christ, along with the bread and the wine. As we have seen in the last chapter, in the parable of the Last Judgment, by a kind of transubstantiation as it were, Jesus identifies himself with the hungry, the thirsty, the stranger, the naked, the prisoner. Just as in the Last Supper he says that the bread is his body and the wine his blood, so in this parable he says that he is they and they are he. Christ is really absent as long as they are not at the table of the Eucharist, eating and drinking with us, as true equals and friends. In the Eucharist, therefore, we not only rejoice in the presence of Christ, we also mourn his absence and ardently long for his coming-in-glory, so long as there is hunger, thirst, sickness, and poverty, so long as strangers and migrants have not become our neighbors and friends, and prisoners have not tasted the joy of freedom.

After the Our Father, the priest recites the following prayer in the name of the community: "Deliver us, Lord, from every evil, and grant us peace in our day. In your mercy keep us free from sin and protect us from all anxiety, as *we wait in joyful hope for the coming of our Savior, Jesus Christ*" (emphasis added). Together with Paul (1 Cor 16:22) and with the author of Revelation, Christians cry out: "*Marana tha!*"—Come, Lord! (Rev 22:20). At his coming, all things will be subjected to Jesus; Jesus will then hand over the kingdom to God the Father "so that God may be all in all" (1Cor 15:28).

11

HOPE

WISHFUL THINKING?

In the first chapter I have suggested that of the three theological virtues, that is, faith, hope, and charity, it is hope that lies at the heart of eschatology. These three virtues appear to correspond loosely to the three questions that, according to the German philosopher Immanuel Kant, are the basic concerns of human reason, both speculative and practical: "What can I know? What ought I to do? What may I hope?" (*Critique of Pure Reason*, 1787). To the first question, Kant answers: We only know the phenomena of things, that is, things as they appear to our senses in the world of time and space, and not the things in themselves. To the second, he says: We ought to do what is right in itself, and not because of its possible rewards, in such a way that our will becomes a universal law (what Kant terms "the categorical imperative"). As to what we can hope, to which he devotes very little attention, Kant says that it is God and life after death. These realities however function for him merely as that which lends coherence and purposiveness to our moral life.

In a certain sense what we Christians hope for can be described in the Kantian terms of God and life after death. There is however a huge difference between these hoped-for realities as they are believed by Christians and what Kant thinks they are, that is, epistemological justifications and warrants for our moral life. Perhaps philosophers as such cannot say anything more than what Kant has said about these objects of human hope, but for Christians, they are not just grounds for ethical behavior but rather what God has said and done in history for God's glory and our eternal happiness, namely, the reign of God, as manifested in human history, in the history of the people of Israel, and above all, in the ministry, death, and resurrection of Jesus. The kingdom of God that will have no end will be fully manifested in Jesus' return in glory to judge the living and the dead and in the resurrection of all humanity, but it is already anticipated and partially realized, as we have seen in the last chapter, in each celebration of the Eucharist.

If the reign of God, often described in the Bible with the most fantastic images, is what Christians hope for, the following questions naturally arise: Is the reign of God an empty projection of the human heart, or is it the fulfillment of the promises of a faithful God who has already carried them out in human history, though not yet fully? Is Christian eschatology what the trio of nineteenth-century German thinkers, Ludwig Feuerbach, Karl Max and Friedrich Engels contend it to be, namely, nothing but wishful thinking, a chimera and an illusion, the desires of the human heart writ large in the sky and ultimately unfulfilled?

If it is not, as we Christians vigorously claim, how can we live the realities of the reign of God here and now? How can we experience the still-to-come eschatological realities of resurrection, judgment, universal reconciliation, and heaven in our daily lives, as realities already truly and really present, and not merely as something that will come only on the other side of our life and at the end of time? How can we show to non-believers that our hope in eternal life is not an empty and vain longing or a doubtful "maybe," but a certainty and conviction born out of God's words and actions in history, of God's promise to do for us all that God has already done for Jesus? How can we find in the "Real Absence" of Christ in the Eucharist a source of inspiration and power to make his "Real Presence" more real, not just in the bread and the wine, but in all people, especially the last and the least and the lost among us, and in all aspects of our life?

I will attempt to answer these questions by exploring the virtue of hope, arguably the least developed of the three theological virtues. Fortunately, several contemporary theologians, for example, Jürgen Moltmann among Protestants, N.T. Wright among Anglicans, and Anthony Kelly among Roman Catholics, have made hope the leitmotif of their eschatologies. Also, Pope Benedict XVI's 2007 encyclical *Spe Salvi* [On Christian Hope] offers deep insights on the virtue of hope and its connection with eschatology.

Wish, Desire, Hope, Expectation

One helpful way to understand the specific shape of the Christian virtue of hope is to see how the four words 'wish,' 'desire,' 'hope,' and 'expect' are normally used in English. 'Wish' is used to express a desire for something one does not currently have, or something that is not easily attainable, or something that is counterfactual, or even for something that is patently impossible. For example, I may say: "I wish I had a billion dollars" (something I do not currently have and will never have, unless Hollywood decides to make a movie out of this little book!) Or: "I wish I will win the lottery next week" (a chance I have since I have bought a lottery ticket, but it is infinitesimally small). Or: "I wish I had studied theoretical physics" (a counterfactual since I have never studied it). Or: "I wish I were thirty years younger" (a physical impossibility since I am a sexagenarian. Note: despite its appearance, the word has nothing to do with being a dirty old man!). It is easy to add a host of other things to this wish list and drop more coins into this wishing well.

There is obviously in these wishes a strong element of what psychologists call "wishful thinking." While wishing for these things, we are aware that these wishes are frivolous, unlikely, and even impossible, and refer to them with the Latinate term 'velleity,' that is, wishes that do not lead to action. Fortunately, if they do not come true, we will not be terribly upset.

'Desire' is a more elemental act than 'wish.' Like 'wish,' desire is directed to something that is not yet present. But unlike 'wish," it springs from the basic instincts and needs of human life such as food, sex, security, beauty, love, or happiness. Desires are more powerful, driven, and obsessive than wishes and are often associated with emotion and passion, and unfortunately, can produce neurotic and psychotic disorders. Unlike wishes, if they are thwarted, humans will experience deep sadness and frustration. Furthermore, though desires that spring from the fundamental needs of human existence are good and their fulfillment contributes to human flourishing, they may become all-consuming and destructive if not brought under control and kept within the bounds of reason and morality. Then, desire transmutes into attachment, craving, greed, lust, and violence. Hence, the goal of ethical and spiritual life is to discipline and eradicate sinful desires, and to channel and direct good ones to promote spiritual growth. In addition to the desires rooted in basic instincts that may be good or evil, there is a desire for God, often experienced by the mystics, a desire that is said to lead to unbounded joy, delight and ecstasy, a desire that makes all other desires superfluous.

Contrary to wish and desire, 'hope' is not an act that is spontaneously initiated by oneself. Rather it is always a response to a promise made by someone else. Thus I do not place my hope in you out of the blue but only because you have made a promise to me, are able to bring it about, and show to have always been true to your word. The solidity of hope depends not on its strength and fervor but on the trustworthiness of the person who makes the promise and on his or her power to fulfill the promise. In fact, the strength of my hope grows in direct proportion to the power of the person who makes the promise and his or her faithfulness. My hope will waver as soon as the person in whom I trust breaks his or her promise or is unable to keep it. Hence, hope is intimately bound with faith and trust. The danger to hope is lack of trust, and its opposite is despair.

Finally, intimately linked with 'hope' is 'expectation.' Expectation is the subjective attitude corresponding to hope. The person who hopes waits for, and expects, the fulfillment of the promise given. If my friend promises to come and visit me, I will eagerly expect and wait for her. But this waiting is not passive; I do not just sit there and do nothing. On the contrary, my waiting for my friend is preceded by house-cleaning and cooking and decorating to make her stay comfortable. While waiting I will occasionally glance out of the window to catch a glimpse of her coming and open the door wide to welcome her before she rings the bell. If she is a bit late, I do not despair; on the contrary, I am certain that she will come because she has always kept her word. My heart is filled with joy and happiness when she finally arrives. Expectation is hope standing on its toes and craning its neck, leaning its body forward and opening its eyes wide, working hard to get everything ready, welcoming and embracing the promised reality when it comes. Expectation is hope marked by preparation, readiness, vigilance, anticipation, waiting, eagerness, patience, endurance, confidence, certitude, joy.

Hope for the Reign of God in the Bible

Turning now to the Bible to understand what the theological virtue of hope is, it will be clear that it has nothing to do with 'wish,' only a little to do with 'desire' and everything to do with 'hope' and 'expectation,' as these terms are explained above. Eschatological hope is not a 'wish,' or more precisely, a velleity, dreaming of the unlikely and the impossible, wishing idly and not acting for what is wished for. In a sense hope is 'desire' since it is a longing for what will fulfill the most basic need of the human heart, namely, life and happiness with God, or as Saint Augustine memorably puts it in his *Confessions*, our heart is restless until it rests in God. Thus life with God is not an add-on or something adventitious or secondary; rather, as another great theologian, Thomas Aquinas, puts it, humans have a *desiderium connaturale* [connatural desire] for God.

But more than anything else, eschatological hope is hope because it is not an act that we perform on our own initiative, by our own effort, and with our own will. Rather the initiative always lies with God; it is God's gift to us, founded on the promise of the faithful God to accomplish in us what God has already accomplished in Christ. It is a waiting in confident hope for God's promises in Christ to be fulfilled in us. It is the other side of faith: Faith trusts in God's promises and hope expects what is to come. God's faithfulness and truthfulness (*emet*) enables us to respond to God's promise with a full-throated shout: "Yes, let it be so!" (*amen*) in confidence and joy.

Hope is repeatedly inculcated by Israel's prophets in the people of God, urging them to "wait for the Lord," calling Yahweh their "hope," and exhorting them to trust in God and not human rulers, as they went through defeats and exiles. Christians believe that Israel's hope for the kingdom of God has been fulfilled in Jesus, though its final and perfect completion is still to come.

Of all the New Testament writers, no one has expressed this eschatological hope more eloquently than Paul. Paul reiterates the Old Testament teaching on hope as trust in God and patient waiting for the fulfillment of God's promise. In his view, this hope is exemplified most powerfully by Abraham. In Paul's words, "hoping against hope, Abraham believed, and thus became the father of many nations" (Rom 4:18). By "hoping against hope" is meant that as his human hope for an offspring through the natural biological processes faded and finally proved impossible due to his and Sarah's advanced age, Abraham's hope did not waver but grew all the stronger as he placed his unconditional trust in God's promise. Thus, for Abraham, God becomes the God of hope.

On the other hand, Paul is convinced that Christ's resurrection marks the fulfillment of God's promise to Israel regarding the kingdom of God and that the presence of the Holy Spirit is evidence of the reality of the end time in our midst. We are now living in the eschatological age. But Christ's glorious resurrection and the outpouring of the Spirit are only the "first fruits" of the new age preparing for and guaranteeing the final stage of God's kingdom in the second coming of Christ to judge the living and the dead. In the meantime, Christians form the new eschatological community, the church, whose distinguishing virtue is hope, living in anticipation of and expecting the full realization of God's purposes for the world, grounded in God's act of salvation in Christ and energized by the power of the Holy Spirit.

Christians, People of Hope

In the strictest sense, then, Christians are a people of hope, and hence their life must be a witness to the hope for the final consummation of all things in God. In his letter to the Romans Paul expresses succinctly how hope must shape Christian life through and through:

> Therefore, since we are justified by faith, we have peace with God through our Lord Jesus Christ, through whom we have obtained access to this grace in which we stand, and we boast in our hope of sharing the glory of God. And not only that, but we also boast in our sufferings, knowing that suffering produces endurance, and endurance produces character, and character produces hope, and hope does not disappoint us, because God's love has been poured into our hearts through the Holy Spirit that has been given to us. (Rom 5:1-5)

There are, in Paul's understanding of Christian hope, two interrelated dimensions: first, an absolute conviction of our sharing in God's peace, grace, and glory, guaranteed by what God has done in Jesus and realized by the Spirit who has been poured into our hearts. Christ is in us "the hope of glory" (Col 1:7). Second, that our complete and perfect sharing in these divine realities still lies in the future, and therefore the virtue we must cultivate is hope, which is born out of character, endurance, and suffering, and which, above all, will not disappoint, not because of our deeds but God's.

In a later part of the same letter, Paul extends this hope beyond humans to include the whole creation:

> For the creation waits with eager longing for the revealing of the children of God; for the creation was subjected to futility, not of its own will but by the will of the one who subjected it, in hope that the creation itself will be set free from its bondage to decay and will obtain the freedom of the glory of the children of God. We know that the whole creation has been groaning in labor pains until now; and not only the creation, but we ourselves, who have the first fruits of the Spirit, groan inwardly while we wait for adoption, the redemption of our bodies. For in hope we were saved. Now hope that is seen is not hope. For who hopes for what is seen? But if we hope for what we do not see, we wait for it with patience. (Rom 8:19-25)

Thus, for Paul hope is the fundamental structure of the whole creation which, together with humanity, like a woman in labor, is groaning toward a new life, that is, the final redemption from sin and death, for it is only in hope that we have been saved.

Living in Hope

The First Letter of Peter begins by blessing God for having given us "a new birth into a living hope through the resurrection of Jesus Christ from the Spirit" (1:3). Later it enjoins: "Always be ready to make your defense to anyone who demands from you an account for the hope that is in you" (3:15). What First Peter has in mind is not simply a theoretical apologetics of the Christian hope. In response to Feuerbach, Marx and Engels, Christians can argue that their hope is not wishful thinking or a vain projection because it is not founded on what humans can achieve but on the promise of a faithful and all-powerful God. Of course, such theoretical response may or may not be persuasive since it rests on a number of other assertions that are not amenable to rational proof, such as God's existence and God's omnipotence and faithfulness.

But there is another way of giving an account of the Christian hope that is persuasive to people of good will, and that is a life lived in hope. I have noted above that Christian hope is expectation. It is not a passive waiting and doing nothing. Rather, hope demands action, the kind of activities that make the objects of Christian hope believable and real. It is not surprising that First Peter ends with exhortations on living a life consistent with the eschatological hope: "The end of all things is near; therefore be serious and discipline yourselves for the sake of your prayers. Above all, maintain constant love for one another, for love covers a multitude of sins. Be hospitable to one another without complaining. Like good stewards of the manifold grace of God, serve one another with whatever gift each of you has received" (4:7-10). Hence, hope must lead to love while "we wait for the blessed hope and the manifestation of the glory of our great God and Savior Jesus Christ" (Titus 2:13).

There are however two conditions of life that call for hope in an urgent way and I would like to conclude with brief reflections on them. The first is illness, in particular the long, debilitating, and painful kinds. Thanks to modern medicine, we can pop pills to reduce pains. But there are illnesses, both physical and psychological, seemingly more widespread in our time, that gradually and irremediably destroy physical mobility, mental faculties, and even spiritual development, such as Alzheimer's and Parkinson's. Without a reasonable prospect of cure, depression and hopelessness sink heavy, not only in the sufferers but also in their loved ones. Of course, not all illnesses are incurable and terminal, and in these cases one may and must take all the necessary measures, though not the extraordinary means, to restore health. In this context it is useful to note that patients with an optimistic attitude and a strong sense of hope have been shown to have a better chance at recovery. In cases of incurable diseases, or especially in the final stages of illness, as I have mentioned in chapter 2, patients should be given hospice care, to minimize physical pains as much as possible, surround them with care and love, and accompany them in the last moments of their lives.

Related to illness is old age. Again, thanks to modern medicine, we live longer, but a longer life does not necessarily add joy and happiness. In many industrialized countries, old age and all its attendant physical and mental conditions of senility represent a serious disability. Our society and culture, geared toward performance and productivity, tend to regard old age as an inconvenience to be tolerated, a problem to be solved, an ugly condition to be kept out of sight in retirement homes and assisted-living centers. Thus, old age becomes the merciless reservation for isolation, neglect, helplessness, loneliness, and despair.

More than ever hope seems to be a much-needed and yet difficult virtue for our time, for the sick as well as the healthy, for the old as well as the young. Glib and pious bromides about offering one's sufferings to God, bearing one's cross in obedience to God's will, and the promise of higher rewards in heaven, albeit well-intentioned, are often worse than useless. Honest and sober acknowledgment of the cruelty of incurable illnesses and humiliating senility are more helpful. Furthermore, as I have argued in chapter 2, in painful and hopeless illness and debilitating old age it is neither sinful to feel anguish nor sacrilegious to cry out to God, as Jesus did: "My God, my God, why have you forsaken me?" (Mk 15:34). In making Jesus' desperate cry our own, we hope that the God who has not abandoned his Son on Good Friday and mysteriously remained silent on Holy Saturday, will come and bring us to a new and transformed life with him on Easter Sunday, as he has done with Jesus. It is a deep irony that the heart of the Christian hope lies in the Easter mystery, the story of Jesus' suffering, death, and resurrection, as there is no more absurd story than this, that of Innocence condemned as

Guilt. And yet, from the abyss of darkness and hatred spring the light and the love that inspire hope for eternal life throughout the whole world.

Of course, since Jesus was killed in the prime of life and the bloom of health, we do not know how he would act in terminal illness and old age, and so we cannot practice "the imitation of Christ," as the fifteenth-century spiritual writer Thomas à Kempis (1380-1471) would have us do, nor can we just say: "What would Jesus do?" Jesus' physical pains, though intense, were short. He was spared the twinge of arthritis, the nausea and vomiting caused by che-motherapy, the bewilderment of Alzheimer's, the tremors of Par-kinson's, the loneliness of old age, the humiliations of senility, the kinds of pain and suffering people of our times are likely to endure. Given the choice, a person may reasonably prefer Jesus' painful yet relatively quick death to lingering and debilitating illnesses.

We must frankly acknowledge that Jesus has not offered us a con-crete model to follow in these tragic conditions. As a human being he was limited by the circumstances of his life and therefore cannot tell us how to behave in these situations as well as in many other things. Still he can teach us a human way to suffer terrible pains. He did experience deep fear at the prospect of his violent death to the point of sweating blood, and he did ask God to spare him the cup of suffering and beg his friends to stay by his side to pray with and for him. Consequently, in going through the pains and sufferings that are the peculiar side-products of modern medicine and technology, we may also humbly admit that we are afraid, and deadly so, pray God to spare us as much as possible of all these suf-ferings and pains, and not hesitate to beg our family and friends to stay with us during the final stage of our earthly pilgrimage.

Willingly or grudgingly, we accept the pains and sufferings of ill-nesses and old age, neither because we fear the punishment of hell nor because we want the reward of heaven. Ultimately, there is only one reason for our hope: God's "everlasting beauty," as the Muslim woman mystic Rābi'ah al-Adawīyah (d. 801) puts it in her prayer, which we Christians can gratefully make our own:

> O God, my whole occupation and all my desire in this world, of all worldly things, is to remember Thee, and in the world to come, is to meet Thee. This is on my side, as I have stated; now do Thou whatsoever Thou wilt. O God, if I worship Thee for fear of Hell, burn me in hell, and if I worship in hope of Paradise, exclude me from Paradise, but if I worship Thee for thy own sake, grudge me not Thy everlasting beauty (A. J. Arberry, *Muslim Saints and Mystics* [London, 1964], 51).

12

THE END OF THE WORLD

A NEW HEAVEN AND A NEW EARTH?

Like everything else, this short book is coming to an end, and it is not a mere coincidence that its last chapter deals with the end of the world and history. Compared with the latter, the end of a book, even of a major classic, let alone a minuscule booklet such as this, is but a drop of water in millions of oceans or a grain of sand on billions of beaches. Still, it is an end and it prompts reflections on "The End."

Perhaps of all the themes discussed in this book, that of the end of the world is the most hypothetical, since what the Bible and Christian Tradition, no less contemporary cosmology, say about it is at best well-founded speculations, at worst Hollywood fictions. Those who take the few biblical texts on how the world will end literalistically, as true-to-fact descriptions of the end-times, have tried to harmonize them, blow-by-blow, with cosmological theories about the end of the physical universe we inhabit and of myriad other possible parallel universes, in order to show that the Bible is as reliable as any modern science.

Before 1998, a group of cosmologists had proposed a theory of the end of the universe, according to which the force of gravity is slowing down the expansion of the universe resulting from the Big Bang some 13.7 billion years ago. At this rate, in another 20 billion years, there will be a Big Crunch in which the universe will shrink, the galaxies merge, the stars explode, and a cosmic conflagration burn up everything. Biblical literalists are quick to point out that such a scenario has been predicted in 2 Peter 3:10-13, which states that "the day of the Lord will come like a thief, and then the heavens will pass away with a loud noise, and the elements will be dissolved with fire, and the earth and everything that is done on it will be disclosed.... The heavens will be set ablaze and dissolved, and the elements will melt with fire."

Science and Religion

Cosmologists have not of course been impressed by the "correspondence" between the biblical "loud noise" and the stellar explosions and between the biblical "fire" and the cosmic heat. Furthermore, it must be noted that such an attempt at harmonizing biblical data with particular scientific hypotheses, is inherently self-defeating since cosmological theories, with which biblical data are made to harmonize, have regularly been disproved and replaced with others as new discoveries are made. For instance, several decades ago cosmologists believed that the universe is slowing down in its expansion since the Big Bang and is contracting as the force of gravity acts to reverse the expansion of the Big Bang, collapsing the universe back to a Big Crunch. As a result, the end of the universe was envisioned as the collapse of all the matter and space-time in the universe into a state of infinite and dimensionless density called "singularity." However, after Edwin Hubble's publication on the recessional velocity of galaxies in 1929 (the Belgian Catholic priest and physicist George Lemaître had published the same discovery two years earlier, in 1927), it is universally agreed that far from slowing down. the expansion of the universe is actually speeding up. Biblical literalists who had been busy making the Bible agree with the picture of a contracting universe were forced to twist the biblical data to fit the new theory of an expanding universe.

More damaging than the necessity of constant revision is the methodological error. Many theologians have noted that this attempt at harmonization between the Bible and science, however well-intentioned, misreads and misuses the biblical texts. Indeed, it has been pointed out that the very text cited in favor of the scientific validity of the Bible in cosmological matters intends to answer a very different sort of question from the ones that concern cosmologists. The context of 2 Peter 3 is not how the world will end but the skepticism about the promised coming of the Lord. "Where is the promise of his coming?" (3:3), the scoffers smirk. True to the apocalyptic genre and using its stock-in-trade imageries, 2 Peter threatens the scoffers, whom it calls "godless" (3:7), with destruction by fire, a typically apocalyptic punishment, and urges Christians to be "patient" at the delay of the day of the Lord and to lead "lives of holiness and godliness, waiting for and hastening the coming of the day of God" (3:11). Most importantly, 2 Peter holds out for those who believe in God's promise the vision of "new heavens and a new earth, where righteousness is at home" (3:13).

The last biblical verse cited above indicates the real issue underlying the dialogue between science and theology, and more narrowly, cosmology and eschatology. It is not the questions of how and when the universe will end, and whether the Bible gives us a sneak preview of the end-time events. Rather it is whether the end of the world, however predicted by contemporary cosmology, sinks us into the deepest despair about the utter futility of creation and human history, or inspires us with the joyful hope of a new heaven and new earth, where "righteousness is at home," and enables us to lead "lives of holiness and godliness."

In other words, is the kingdom of God, which Jesus inaugurated and which is now coming in its fullness, a new heaven and a new earth, not a destruction or a total replacement of this world, but *this very same world* transformed into what God intends it to be?

Furthermore, if the new heaven and the earth are no other than *this* heaven and *this* earth, what is the precise connection between the two? Is there "continuity," or "discontinuity," or both between the two? Can the "first creation" be understood without reference to the "new creation" and vice versa? Will space-time and matter remain in the new creation, and if so, are they identical with what they were in the first creation? Is the new creation the product of human ingenuity and work, or is it the work of God who is faithful to God's promises?

Answers to these questions must be rooted in the Bible as far as possible, even though the issues bedeviling contemporary cosmologists may not be, and often are not, the same as those of the Bible. As an example, let us look at the last vision of the seer in the last book of the Bible, namely, Revelation:

> Then I saw a new heaven and a new earth; the first heaven and the first earth had passed away, and the sea was no more. And I saw the holy city, the new Jerusalem, coming down out of heaven from God, prepared as a bride adorned for her husband. And I heard a loud voice from the throne saying, "See, the home of God is among mortals. He will dwell with them, they will be his peoples, and God himself will be with them. He will wipe every tear from their eyes. Death will be no more; mourning and crying and pain will be no more, for the first things have passed away (Rev 21:1-4).

Again, were we to take this text as a cosmological theory or an advance report of what the new heaven and a new earth will look like, scientists and cosmologists will have a field day with embarrassing questions: Where will the so-called first heaven and first earth go? To another and perhaps, parallel universe? If the sea will be no more, where and how will the waters of the seas be disposed of? Will there be other oceans elsewhere? How big is the new Jerusalem? Will there be in it buildings, trees, animals and other organic and inorganic stuffs that make up cities? How will it descend from heaven? Fast or slow? The loud voice from heaven: in what language will it be? If death will be no more, will people live forever? What kind of bodies will there be if they are not subject to growth, decay and dissolution? Well, you can add your own questions to join in the fun.

As I have argued throughout this book, these biblical texts, with their fantastic images and language, belong to the literary genre known as apocalyptic and should be read accordingly. They are not description, prediction, or report. Rather they express a vision, or better, the hope of a world totally under the rule of God—a world of justice, peace, abundance, well-being, harmony for all—which is not an *u-topia*, literally, no place, but an *eu-topia*, literally, a good place. It is a good place because it is a new creation of the loving and good God to transform the first creation that has been marred by sin and not a product of fallen humanity.

In reading these biblical texts, therefore, we have to carry out the three hermeneutical tasks I have mentioned in several of the previous chapters. That is, we must try to find out answers to three questions: What is the world *behind* the text? What is the world *in* the text? And, what is the world *in front of* the text? Hopefully by the end of our considerations of these three issues we will have a good understanding of what the new heaven and new earth stand for. But before exploring these three issues let's take a quick view of various cosmological theories about the end of the universe.

Will the Universe End in Nothingness?

My intention here is not to present the various cosmological theories about the end of the universe. I am in no way qualified to do this; I barely made it through *Astronomy for Dummies* and *The Complete Idiot's Guide to Theories of the Universe*. My ignorance in these cosmological matters is deeper than black holes. Fortunately, it is not too difficult to understand what cosmologists hypothesize about how the universe will "end"—or will not end, as the case might be—and what they say is not much more than hypotheses that are being constantly challenged, modified, fine-tuned, and even rejected. In other words, we can imagine the various scenarios of the end of the universe as postulated by cosmologists and astrophysicists without having to grasp all their extremely complex arguments for one theory rather than another. Our task then is not to examine the scientific validity of the various scenarios, which is beyond our ability and purpose. Rather, of each scenario of the end of the universe we will ask whether it bespeaks the utter and final futility of human history and the emptiness, purposelessness and pointlessness of the universe, or whether there is within these scenarios something that points to a "new creation," a "new heaven and a new earth," for which we must hope and work.

In the monthly journal *Atlantic* July/August 2013 issue, thirteen noted scientists and thinkers are invited to answer the question: "How and when will the world end?" Of course, the answers vary enormously, depending on the respondents' scientific expertise and personal interests. I will report here only some answers from a variety of respondents. Gerta Keller, a Princeton University paleontologist, says: "Four of five extinctions in history were driven by volcanic eruptions that flooded entire continents. Our world could quite possibly end with the explosive eruption of Yellowstone, which is past due." Nathaniel Rich, the author of *Odds Against Tomorrow*, declares: "During this century, odds are that we'll see a global pandemic, the destruction of Seattle and San Francisco by earthquakes, the catastrophic flooding of New York, and the assassination of a sitting U.S. president. But most dangerous would be an exchange of nuclear weapons. Probability tables suggest that this is likely to occur by 2082." The astrophysicist Neil deGrasse Tyson, of the American Museum of Natural History, predicts: "The world will be here, with or without us, until the sun dies, 5 billion years hence. At that point, the sun's atmosphere will have expanded to engulf the entire orbit of Mercury, Venus, and earth, which will have become charred embers, spiraling one by one to the crucible that is the sun's core. Have a nice day." The nuclear scientist Taylor Wilson says: "I think it'll be what we don't see coming—a killer asteroid, a nearby gamma-ray burst, or a solar event. All the better reason to become a spacefaring species!" Natalie Angier, science writer for the *New York Times*, opines: "Life has persisted on Earth for nearly 4 billion years. The average mammalian species, on the other hand, lasts just 1 million years. So for you, me, and our 7 billion compatriots, it will be all over by the year 2129." The spiritual writer Deepak Chopra suggests: "The end of the world will come about as a result of misunderstanding that we and the world are separate. Tidal waves will flood coastal landmasses, resulting in millions of refugees, violence, warfare, and chaos. The earth will become a boiling cauldron. The human experiment will have failed." Finally, Ray Kurzweil, director of engineering, Google, is quite laconic: "In the (unlikely) event that we decide to end it."

I am very pleased that you can only read my text and not see me. If you could, you will notice my selfishly happy face in spite of the dire predictions of the cataclysmic destruction of the universe and humanity. The reason is that according to the most authoritative scientists, the end of the world will occur 5 billion years from now, or in 2120, or as early as 2082, the calculation of the dates varying enormously. At any rate, in any of these scenarios I will have most likely long been gone and will watch the spectacular events of the end-times safely from afar, hopefully not in hell, probably in purgatory, and prayerfully in heaven! My reaction reminds me that of an old lady in a (presumably apocryphal) story who was deeply terrified by a lecture on the end of the universe in which there was talk of the contraction of the universe into a Big Crunch, the death of the sun, the resulting Big Freeze, and the disappearance of the universe into black holes. She was however immensely relieved when the lecturer assured her that this cosmic scenario, if it happens at all, will take place perhaps in twenty billion years.

Joking aside, there is a chilling note in a couple of the experts' comments, especially by Deepak Chopra and Ray Kurzweil, which highlight human responsibility for the end of the Earth, whatever and whenever the "far-future universe" will emerge. It is best captured in Kurzwell's one-liner: "In the (unlikely) event that we decide to end it [the world]." I will come back to this point toward the end of this chapter. For now, to be noted is the pervasive and profound pessimism in the above-quoted comments by scientists and thinkers about the meaning, purpose, and intrinsic worth not only of humanity but also of the universe itself.

This pessimism is evident in all the scenarios of the end of the Earth, and on a larger scale, of the universe itself that have been envisaged by contemporary cosmologists. First, with regard to the end of the Earth, one scenario attributes its end to human misuse of natural resources together with environmental destruction by the dumping of waste, air and water pollution, global warming, and the destruction of the ozone layer. Another sees the threat of the destruction of the Earth by its possible collision with comets and asteroids that brings about mass extinctions and sea-level changes. The third scenario envisages the death of the sun in five billion years when it will have exhausted its available hydrogen fuel and its center will become a white dwarf, an object of high density about the size of the Earth. As the result of the sun's death which no longer provides heat and light, the Earth will become uninhabitable, and human life will end, unless humans migrate to and colonize other planets for survival.

Concerning the end of the universe itself, I have already mentioned above the early hypothesis, now abandoned, of the contracting and slowing-down universe, with its corresponding scenario of the end of the universe, namely, the collapse of the universe back to a Big Crunch. Cosmologists speculated whether after the Big Crunch another universe will "bounce" into a new Big Bang, and thus the process of expansion and contraction will go on indefinitely, in a cyclic or oscillatory movement.

Since 1998, however, the discovery of supernovae convinced cosmologists that far from slowing down, the universe is actually speeding up. To account for this fact they postulate the existence of a material or force responsible for the universe's accelerating rate of expansion and refer to it as "dark energy," the existence of which is confirmed by the Wilkinson Microwave Anisotropy Probe. One surprising feature of this dark energy, which makes up 73 percent of the universe (cold dark matter constituting 23 percent, and atoms 4 percent), is that it does not attract gravity but repels it. Because of this repulsion force, the universe is accelerating in its rate of expansion. How exactly dark energy acts to propel the expansion of the universe is the subject of much speculation, but of the expansion of the universe there is now widespread agreement among cosmologists.

In the model of the universe with "eternal expansion" its end is pictured as follows: When the universe is one trillion years old (it is now 13.7 billion years old), new stars cease to form and all the old massive stars, which will have exhausted their supply of hydrogen fuel, turn into neutron stars and black holes. At 100 trillion years, small stars become white dwarfs. The universe then reaches a state of maximum entropy and a temperature minimum and becomes a cold place, composed of dead stars and black holes. It is in a "Big Freeze" or "Heat Death." Eventually matter itself will decay under the radioactive influence; nothing will be left but some weakly interacting particles and a low-level energy background.

As David Wilkinson points out, "In fact there may be an even more pessimistic future for the Universe. If the Universe came from 'nothing' could an ever-expanding Universe with an infinite future go back to nothing?" (David Wilkinson, *Christian Eschatology and the Physical Universe* [New York: Bloomsbury T&T Clark, 2010], 16).

The prospect of the total destruction of the Earth, and with it human history, due to human abuses of natural resources, or the accidental collision with comets and asteroids, or the certain death of the sun, and of the eventual annihilation of the universe itself in a Big Freeze or Heat Death, poses severe challenges to the Christian belief in God the creator, God's providence, the eternal destiny of humanity, and above all, the eschatological hope in the kingdom of God. Everything in the history of the Earth and the universe as a whole relentlessly and ruthlessly bespeaks utter and final meaninglessness, pointlessness, and futility.

Is there a way out of this pessimism and hopelessness on the basis of science? One can perhaps derive some comfort from the fact that at least through science we can *understand* that the universe has no point, and that this itself is the *meaning* of the universe, that is, it has no meaning, no purpose, no goal, no fulfillment, at least as far as science can tell. To know *that* is arguably already a meaningful achievement. Or, secondly, we can speculate, with some cosmologists, that there will be a "Big Bounce," that is, once this universe collapses under the Big Freeze or Heat Death, it will spawn another universe through another Big Bang, and the process is repeated endlessly, in an oscillatory universe, or a cyclic repetition of an infinite number of Big Bangs. Or, thirdly, we can follow other cosmologists who theorize that our universe is only one possible universe emerging out of the Big Bang. If, instead of assuming that during its first stage of existence the entire universe passed from the inflationary state to the non-inflationary state at a single time, we accept the "eternal inflation" model according to which different parts of the universe passed from the inflationary to the non-inflationary state at different times. Then it is possible to postulate the existence of a "multiverse," a plurality of parallel universes, so that even if our universe reaches heat death, there are other universes that do not, and thus the multiverse as a whole will never end.

I must admit however that neither the clear-eyed scientific knowledge of the pointlessness of the universe, nor the speculations about the "Big Bounce," nor the theory of the "multiverse" bring any soothing balm to my depression about the fate of human history and the universe. As the famous cosmologist Carl Sagan has said, "There is no reason to deceive ourselves with pretty stories for which there's little good evidence. Far better it seems to me, in our vulnerability, is to look at death in the eye and to be grateful every day for the brief but magnificent opportunity that life provides" (Carl Sagan, *Billions and Billions: Thoughts on Life and Death at the Brink of the Millennium* [New York: Random House Ballantine Books, 1997], 215).

Sagan's point is well-taken, especially if the "pretty stories" refers to speculations about events that may or may not happen thousands of trillions of years from now. Indeed, it is perfectly rational for cosmologists, *qua* cosmologists, to be atheists, or at least agnostics, as indeed quite a few of them are. On the evidence of science *alone*, whatever little of it is available, atheism and agnosticism seem to be the only reasonable and intellectually honest options, and faith in the ultimate meaning of the universe, however it is couched, is nothing but wishful thinking or "opium for the masses."

Fortunately, the "pretty stories" may also refer to narratives other than cosmological speculations. They are stories for which "there's little good evidence," if by evidence is meant *scientific* and *empirical* proofs. But, as I have argued in chapter 1, human knowledge is not based exclusively on empirical proofs; otherwise, life would be deadly boring, and *human* life impossible. After all, we do not live by bread (or rice) alone! These stories are transmitted mainly in religious traditions, and so, as Christians, we turn to the "pretty stories" of the Bible to see if there is a way out of this morass of skepticism and meaninglessness.

The Bible on the End of the Universe

At first sight recourse to the Bible does not seem to be a wise move. As it turns out, the Holy Book is not without texts of dark cynicism and despair. Ecclesiastes opens with the celebrated lines: "Vanity of vanities, says the Teacher, vanity of vanities! All is vanity.... All is vanity and a chasing after wind" (1:1, 15). Perhaps not even the most ardent agnostic and atheistic cosmologist can match the Teacher's eloquence on the futility of life. Ironically, these words, which occur like a mantra throughout the text, come from the mouth of one who claims that "I have acquired great wisdom, surpassing all who were over Jerusalem before me; and my mind had great experience of wisdom and knowledge" (1:16).

Note that, according to the Teacher, futility of life is the lesson he learns from "great wisdom," the ancient equivalent of "science" today. But the Teacher is also aware that there is another source of knowledge, namely, God: "To the one who pleases him God gives wisdom and knowledge and joy" (2:26). Later on, he says: "I know that whatever God does endures forever; nothing can be added to it, nor anything taken away from it; God has done this, so that all should stand in awe before him" (3:14). Of course, the Teacher is no cosmologist, and his conviction that "whatever God does endures forever" does not provide him with special insights on how the universe will end. Nevertheless, the advice he gives, which he repeats frequently, is not very far from Sagan's wise counsel, though his motive is very different: "Go, eat your bread with enjoyment, and drink your wine with a merry heart, for God has long ago approved what you do" (9:7).

For a biblical view on how the universe will end we have to turn to other texts. I have already cited above two of them: 2 Pet 3:10-13 and Rev 21:1-8. Two other texts, 1 Thess 4:13-5:11, was discussed in chapters 1 and 8, and Rom 8:18-30 in chapter 11. Other significant texts include Isa 11:1-9 and Isa 65:17-25. When interpreting these texts, as I have already mentioned, we must avoid the methodological blunder of reading them literalistically and looking for "correspondences" between the details these texts are purported to give on the end of the universe and the various scenarios contemporary cosmologists have postulated. As has been argued above, it would be a self-defeating task.

It is not possible to do a detailed exegesis of the three texts not already discussed. For the reader's convenience, I will cite their most important verses here:

> *The wolf shall live with the lamb,*
> *The leopard shall lie down with the kid,*
> *The calf and the lion and the fatling together.*
> *And a little child shall lead them.*
> *The cow and the bear shall graze,*
> *their young shall lie down together,*

and the lion shall eat straw like the ox.
The nursing child shall play over the hole of the asp,
and the weaned child shall put its hand on the adder's den.
They will not hurt or destroy on all my holy mountain;
for the earth will be full of the knowledge of the Lord
as the water covers the sea. (Isa 11:6-9)

For I am about to create new heavens and a new earth,
the former things shall not be remembered or come to mind.
But be glad and rejoice forever in what I am creating;
for I am about to create Jerusalem as a joy,
and its people as a delight. (Isa 65:17-18)

I consider that the sufferings of this present time are not worth comparing with the glory about to be revealed to us. For the creation waits with eager longing for the revealing of the children of God; for the creation is subjected to futility, not of its own will but by the will of the one who subjected it, in hope that the creation itself will be set free from its bondage to decay and will obtain the freedom of the children of God. We know that the whole creation has been groaning in labor pains until now, and not only the creation, but we ourselves, who have the first fruits of the Spirit, groan inwardly while we wait for adoption, the redemption of our bodies. For in hope we were saved. Now hope that is seen is no hope. For who hopes for what is seen? But if we hope for what we do not see, we wait for it with patience. (Rom 8:18-25)

The first thing to be said about these texts as well as the others already discussed is that they have absolutely nothing to do with cosmological speculations about the end of the Earth and the universe, similar to the end-of-time scenarios I have summarized above. It would be utterly foolish to put them side by side and look for similarities and correspondences. They are, to use a modern term, "parallel universes." The first two texts from Isaiah do not speak of the end of the cosmos but present an idyllic and charming picture of the future Israel in its perfect state of union with God.

Nor is the text from Romans to be construed as a theory about the end of the universe, and no attempt should be made under any circumstance to correlate its images of the "sufferings of the present time," of creation being "subjected to futility," of its "being set free from its bondage to decay," and its "groaning in labor pains" to the universe's increasing rate of expansion through dark energy, the gradual decay of matter through entropy, the death of the sun and the stars, and the lifelessness of the universe under the Big Freeze and Heat Death.

This does not mean that these texts have nothing to say to us about what we may and must hope for the universe and for ourselves. But to discover this meaning we must turn to the three by now familiar questions: What is the world *behind* the text? What is the world *in* the text? What is the world *in front of* the text?

Turning now to the first question: "What is the world *behind* the text?" of the biblical texts about the end of the world, it bears repeating, given the wide misuse of them in the circle of literalist interpreters to forecast the Doomsday, that clearly it is not that of scientific cosmology and astrophysics, for the simple reason that the sacred writers knew less than nothing about them. Nor, more importantly, was it their interest. Before we explain this point, it is to be noted in passing that the contemporary scientific language about the end of the world pales in comparison with the spectacular and fanciful images the Bible uses with reference with the end of the world. The image of the death of the universe by the Big Freeze or Heat Death is ridiculously tame in comparison with the biblical images of wars and rumors of war, famines, earthquakes, the darkening of the sun and the moon, the falling of the stars, the shaking of the powers of heaven, the sounding of trumpets by angels, and the gathering of the elects from the four winds, from one end of heaven to the other, the defeat of the dragon by the archangel Michael, the plagues, the battle of Satan and his angels, the appearance of the antichrist, and so on. This plethora and diversity of hair-raising images and languages should alert readers to the fact that the Bible is not interested in predicting and describing the end of the world, as the *Atlantic* has asked various scientists to do. It is therefore meaningless and useless to try to match the biblical images of the darkening of the sun and the moon and the stars with the cosmological hypotheses of the death of the universe by gradual contraction or by eternal expansion.

To put the matters concisely and starkly, the biblical vision of the end of the world is ironically not about the world but about *the God of the world*. It is not about natural and cosmic cataclysms but a profession of faith, hope, and love in the power of the God who will not abandon those whom the political and economic powers of the world, more specifically the Roman empire, have oppressed and killed. This world of injustice, oppression, killing, violence, imperial hegemony against the weakest and innocent members of the human family is the world *behind* the text of the biblical descriptions of the end of the world, especially in Revelation. It is a voice of protest, an act of subversion, a movement of rebellion against the political, economic and religious powers-that-be that claim to possess divine authority and to stand in the place of God. It is therefore ultimately a condemnation of idolatry. It is a profession of hope that this idolatrous world—the "first heaven and the first earth"—will be destroyed, not by us but by God. It is God himself who will bend down to dry the tears and remove the pains of these victims of injustice and violence. Or as the Teacher in Ecclesiastes puts it with supreme confidence: "I know that whatever God does endures forever; nothing can be added to it, nor anything taken away from it; God has done this, so that all should stand in awe before him."

Secondly, the world *in* the text is not that of ecological disasters and cosmic cataclysms, of collision of comets and killer asteroids, of volcanic eruptions and coastal tsunamis, of earthquakes and tornados. Rather it is the world populated by Roman emperors and military leaders, political and cultural establishments, religious authorities and legal experts, financial corporations and business executives on the one hand, and the "poor of Yahweh" on the other, those who have no one and nothing to rely on except what God has done for Jesus and God's promise that God will do for them what

God has done for Jesus. To be more precise, *we ourselves* are the people constituting the world *in* the text, since we can be modern-day Roman authorities and military leaders, religious authorities and legal experts, CEOs of financial organizations and multinational corporations, who stand to benefit much from economic globalization on the back of the poorest of the poor and to the destruction of the environment.

Thirdly, as to the world *in front of* the text, it is high-time to heed what the scientists say about human responsibility in ending the world. The role of humans in destroying the world, usurping a divine prerogative and thus an act of hubris and idolatry, reveals the world *in front of* the text of the apocalyptic literature. It opens up a new way of being and acting in the world and beckons us to acknowledge our status as creatures and fulfill our tasks as stewards of God's creation. In this way we join in God's work for justice and peace and reconciliation, to "mend the world" (the Jewish concept of *tikkun olam*). Biblically, the end of the world is not to be understood as the inevitable and irreversible course of entropy but the deed of a loving and just God who will restore the world to its original justice and will transform it into the "new heaven and the new earth." It is here that the two texts from Isaiah cited above no longer read like naive projections or idyllic poetry—in which world do wolves lie down with lambs, bears eat grass like cows, and lions eat straw like oxen? Rather they act as a theological manifesto challenging our imagination to envision a time and a place—an *eu-topia*—where "the earth is full of the knowledge of Lord as the waters cover the sea" and to *act* upon this vision.

The New Heaven and the New Earth

The seer of Revelation waxes highly poetic in depicting the new heaven and the new earth. He reports the words of the one sitting on the throne declaring: "See, I am making all things new" (21:5). Then he mentions the holy city Jerusalem coming out of heaven from God and "has the glory of God and a radiance like a very rare jewel, like jasper, clear as crystal. Then he says that he sees no temple in the city, "for its temple is the Lord God the Almighty and the Lamb. And the city has no need of sun or moon to shine on it, for the glory of God is its light, and its lamp is the Lamb" (21:22-23).

How is this new Jerusalem coming down from heaven related to the old Jerusalem? Or, more generally, how is this present world related to the new heaven and the new earth symbolized by the New Jerusalem? Is there *continuity* between the "first creation" and the "new creation"? Or, is there total *discontinuity* between them, such that the old universe will be destroyed and *replaced* by another one? Or, is there *continuity in discontinuity* such that the new creation is *this same* first creation that is transformed, not by our actions but by an act of God?

The answer I favor is the third: the same universe but transformed, not by humans but by God, continuity-in-discontinuity, or more exactly, more-discontinuity-than-continuity. The best analogy to understand this reality of the new heaven and the new earth is the resurrected body of Jesus, as I have explained in chapter 8. It is the body born of Mary, the body in which Jesus lived and was killed, and which still bears the marks of his wounds, but it is a body that his disciples, who had known him well, could not recognize despite an absence of barely three days. Mary Magdalen mistook him for a gardener; the disciples thought he was a ghost. It is a body that is no longer bound by space and time. It is nonetheless the same Jesus, whom the disciples on the way to Emmaus recognized in the breaking of bread.

Here I would like to propose another analogy. In my reflections on the Eucharist in chapter 10 as a foretaste of eternal life I suggested that the bread and the wine are not destroyed or replaced by something else but acquire a new "meaning" and a new "end," while preserving the characteristics of bread and wine. In an analogous way, I suggest, our world—human and cosmic—will not be destroyed at the end of time but will receive a new meaning and a new end. To use the language of traditional Eucharistic theology, we could say that the "substance" of our present world will be "transubstantiated" into the new heaven and the new earth by the power of the Holy Spirit, while retaining the characteristics or "accidents" of this world. We can still recognize our present world in the new heaven and the new earth, and at the same time know that it has been transformed in its meaning ("transsignification") and its end ("transfinalization"). It is perhaps not possible to go beyond this rather general statement as a theological assertion, but of course our imagination can roam free and conjure up all kinds of things that gladden and delight our senses, minds, and hearts.

The Second Vatican Council uses a sober language to expresses this hope of the transformation and consummation of the world. To my knowledge, there is no magisterial statement that expresses in greater depth and beauty both the continuity and discontinuity, preservation and transformation of the universe at the end of time than paragraph 39 of its Pastoral Constitution on the Church in the Modern World (*Gaudium et Spes*). There is no better way to end this book than citing this text in full:

> We do not know the moment of the consummation of the earth and of humanity nor the way the universe will be transformed. The form of this world, distorted by sin, is passing away and we are taught that God is preparing a new dwelling and a new earth in which righteousness dwells, whose happiness will fill and surpass all the desires of peace arising in human hearts. Then death will have been conquered, the daughters and sons of God will be raised in Christ and what was sown in weakness and dishonor will become incorruptible; charity and its works will remain and all creation, which God made for humanity, will be set free from its bondage to decay.
>
> We have been warned, of course, that it profits us nothing if we gain the whole world and lose or forfeit ourselves. Far from diminishing our concern to develop this earth, the expectation of a new earth should spur us on, for it is here that the body of a new human family grows, foreshadowing in some way the age which is to come. That is

why, although we must be careful to distinguish earthly progress clearly from the increase of the kingdom of
Christ, such progress is of vital concern to the kingdom of
God, insofar as it can contribute to the better ordering of
human society.

When we have spread on earth the fruits of our nature
and our enterprise—human dignity, sisterly and broth-
erly communion, and freedom—according to the command
of the Lord and in his Spirit, we will find them once again,
cleansed this time from the stain of sin, illuminated and
transfigured, when Christ presents to his Father an eternal and universal kingdom of truth and life, a kingdom of
holiness and grace, a kingdom of justice, love and peace.
Here on earth the kingdom is mysteriously present, when
the Lord comes it will enter into its perfection.

EPILOGUE

ENVOI

AN UNFINISHED ENDING?

The above title, which contains an oxymoron, is deliberately ambiguous. The word *envoi* means the concluding words, such as the short stanza ending a ballad or the epilogue of a book. The remaining pages of this book are in this sense an envoi, an archaic term for an afterword. Moreover, envoi, being the *last* word, may also mean an authoritative, indisputable, and definitive statement on a particular subject, with nothing further to add. By its very nature no assertion on the "Last Things" can be an envoi in this sense. No apodictic argument of the "been there, done that" kind can be mounted to prove the veracity of one's statements and close off the discussion. Thus, an envoi in a book on eschatology cannot be but an "unfinished ending," an inevitable yet felicitous oxymoron.

In this open-ended ending I do not intend to—nor indeed can I—offer a set of irreformable dogmatic formulations on the Last Things. There are of course realities about death and eternal life that form part of the Christian faith—the "deposit of faith," to use an older, quaint expression—to which Christians are committed to giving an irrevocable assent. However, every theological elaboration of these realities remains in principle subject to revision and improvement. In this envoi as "unfinished ending" I will highlight some of the key concepts that undergird my foregoing reflections on the Last Things, while inviting further explorations and even differing interpretations of these ever-elusive issues.

Some readers pick up this book on eschatology with the hope that it will provide answers to issues touching the deepest parts of their lives, while others do so out of mere curiosity about what the afterlife, if there be such, will look like. To begin with, to both groups I recommend that when speaking about the Last Things, we mightily resist the urge to find *information* of the kind that can be verified by empirical evidence about what happens in and after death, especially when we turn to the Bible as source of information. The Bible is not intended to provide us with *additional* information to supplement and, when called for, correct what science tells us about these realities, as if the Bible contains scientific *information* that is exclusively available from divine revelation, on realities that lie beyond the competence of science. The books of Scripture, as the Second Vatican Council declares, "firmly, faithfully, and without error, teach that truth which God, *for the sake of our salvation,* wished to see confided to the sacred scriptures" (*Dogmatic Constitution on Divine Revelation,* §11, emphasis added). The Bible does not—and I would add, cannot—provide facts and figures, a journalistic report as it were, on the afterlife, to satisfy our intellectual curiosity, and it would be a gross distortion of its nature and purpose were we to look for this kind of information in it.

This does not mean that faith/religion and reason/science are mutually contradictory. On the contrary, especially with regard to eschatology, together with the "scientific imagination" that proceeds from data gathering to hypothesis formulation, empirical verification, theory construction, and practical application, we need the "eschatological imagination" by which we project onto our human destiny what has occurred in Jesus of Nazareth. Jesus' ministry-death-resurrection-ascension-return functions as the hermeneutical key to unfold the meaning of our death and dying and our life after death. To encapsulate it in a slogan, eschatology is the Christologization of anthropology.

In general, then, if life is imagined as a journey, it must be said that we Christians more or less know how it has started, even on a cosmic scale, that is, in God's creative act, and where it will end, again on a cosmic scale, that is, in the reign of God, but we do not have concrete and detailed information on how this journey will unfold, for us as individuals at death and for the cosmos as a whole at the end of history. We know that life is living into death, and death may lead into life, but we have no absolute certainty that by "living into death" we will "die into life." We do not of course undertake our life journey in the dark and without a leader to guide our steps. Jesus' words and deeds are the map showing us the way, but the map, to use a hackneyed phrase, is not the territory. We live not by sight but by faith, as Saint Paul reminds us (2 Cor 5:7). In turn, faith in the afterlife transmutes into *hope*, in the sense of *expectation* (*prosdokōmen*/*expectamus*), or looking *forward* to—and not "looking *for*," as the current official English translation of the Nicene-Constantinopolitan Creed badly puts it—the resurrection of the dead and life everlasting. Expectation is hope-standing-on-its-toes, actively working for the kingdom of God.

With this ever-vigilant and confident hope/expectation, we can turn to the pages of the Bible, and using all the scholarly resources available we try to interpret it as a historical record of God's dealings with humanity, as a literary work, and as a collection of inspired and sacred books. With regard to its eschatological texts, we take them as part of the literary genre known as apocalyptic literature, and try to discern the world *behind*, *in*, and *in front of* them.

In light of biblical teachings on the Last Things, we can understand how dying can be both the natural and inevitable end of biological life and an event that *I*, and not someone else, must face, with fear and trembling, as a threat of total destruction of my whole self and not just my body. On the other hand, I am given the grace to die as Jesus did, in despair at being abandoned by God *and* in trust in the faithful God who will take my life in his hands. So I will not die alone, and consequently must do my best to help others die also not alone but surrounded with care and love.

Meanwhile I must try "to live into death" so as to be able "to die into life," and the source of this way of living is the hope for heaven and simply not the fear of hell. Heaven and hell are not parallel options God creates for us. God only offers us heaven, which is nothing but eternal life with God and with all humanity in a transformed universe; by refusing this offer I create hell for myself. Heaven is the reality; hell is a possibility, a serious one indeed, first of all for me. Christian faith does not permit us to categorically affirm that there is no hell. Nevertheless, we may and must hope and pray that there will ultimately be no such thing for anyone, trusting that God's infinite and all-merciful love will, like the sun, melt the iciest of hearts and burn the last trace of evil and sin and embrace us all in God's kingdom.

At the heart of Christian hope is the expectation of life everlasting and the resurrection of the dead. Life everlasting consists in knowing God with the knowledge with which God knows Godself, directly and immediately, and not through some created medium, and a sharing in the life of the Triune God: Father, Son, and Spirit. It is also a perfect communion with all other human beings, not only with members of our family, friends and acquaintances, but with each and every person who has ever lived, from the first human being that emerged out of the mists of evolution to the last person on earth. This cosmic homecoming will take place because what we "expect" is not just the immortality of our souls but the resurrection of the dead. It is something that staggers our imagination, as it should be, since it is an act of God's recreation of *this* cosmos into a new heaven and a new earth.

As we wait in joyful hope for this dawning of God's reign and Christ's return in glory to judge the living and the dead, we as members of the body of which Christ is the head gather together to celebrate the Eucharist, a symbol, that is, a sign and instrument, of Christ's presence among us *and* simultaneously his absence. Because of Christ's real presence in the Eucharist we truly are nourished by his body and blood, that is, all that Christ has ever said, done, and been, his very self, human and divine; by his absence we are urged and beckoned to look forward to, with eager hearts and works of love, his Parousia, or glorious manifestation, at which Christ will destroy the last enemy that is death and then hand over his kingdom to God the Father "so that God may be all in all" (1 Cor 15:28).

It is also this hope for God's final victory and lordship over all things that sustains us as we listen to the various cosmological theories about the end of the universe. However the universe will end, the Christian story, as realized supremely in the death-and-resurrection of Jesus, allows us to hope that human history and the universe will have final meaning and not despair over their ultimate absurdity. This is so because the biblical vision of the end of the world is not about the end of the *world* but about the *God* of the world, not about what *humans* will have achieved but about what *God* will do out of faithfulness to God's promises that he has fulfilled in Jesus. Thus, the seer in the last book of the Bible speaks of the "new heaven and the new earth," which is not another, totally new creation but *this* universe, now purified and transformed, not by human hands but by God's infinite power and love.

So here is the dawning of the unended ending. It is the *end* of my life, of human history, and of the physical universe. These ends can in principle be documented, by the tombstone, the last pages of history books, the cosmological predictions. But it is an *unended* ending, something that cannot however be proved or disproved by scientific experiments, nor can the envoi ever be spoken on it; instead, it can only be hoped for. This hope is no idle wish, or vague desire, or the soothing opium for the masses. It is based on what God has done for Jesus of Nazareth, and we hope against hope to the end (Rom 4:18) that God will do it for you and me and all human beings.

ACKNOWLEDGMENTS

I would like to thank Michael Bloom, founder of *Now You Know Media*, for his generous permission to publish in print the series of lectures that his company recorded in CDs. Readers who prefer listening to rather than reading my text can easily order the CDs by visiting the company's website.

I also am deeply grateful to Dr. Brennan Hill, founder of Lectio Publishing and a long-time friend, for his enthusiastic reception of my manuscript. I dreaded and at the same time welcomed his emails which beneath the gentle ribbing and tongue-in-cheek assurances of "no pressure" there was the patient and encouraging query: When are you sending me your manuscript? I also thank Eric Wolf, of the same company, for his editorial work and for reminding me of Romans 15:4: "For whatever was written previously was written for our instruction, that by endurance and by the encouragement of the scriptures we might have hope."

Finally, to those friends who were worried about my—in their view—morbid interest in death and dying and urged me to get a life (if a bit late), I promise I won't write another book on "eschatology."

CPSIA information can be obtained at www.ICGtesting.com
Printed in the USA
BVOW09s1135261114

376890BV00005B/9/P